IMAGES
of England

DOVER

A welcome arch in Biggin Street in 1869 when a 16,000 strong defence force descended on Dover for an Easter Monday exercise. The cameraman was facing St Martin's Terrace, which is now a row of shops opposite the town hall. A hurricane caused the loss of the training brig *Ferret*, smashed to pieces against a pier, but fortunately all eighty-six boys on board and twenty crew abandoned ship. In spite of this event, the exercise went on, watched by Prince Arthur, the Duke of Cambridge and Lord Granville who rode from Walmer Castle to see it.

IMAGES
of England

DOVER

Compiled by
Bob Hollingsbee

TEMPUS

First published 2000
reprinted 2002
Copyright © Bob Hollingsbee, 2000

Tempus Publishing Limited
The Mill, Brimscombe Port,
Stroud, Gloucestershire, GL5 2QG

ISBN 0 7524 1622 7

Typesetting and origination by
Tempus Publishing Limited
Printed in Great Britain by
Midway Colour Print, Wiltshire

Waterloo Crescent and the Promenade feature in this fine mid-nineteenth century lithograph by W.R. Waters for Dover publisher George Warren, of the Marine Library, Marine Parade. Warren dedicated this engraving from the original drawing to Benjamin Eveleigh Winthrop Esq. who lived at No. 8 Marine Parade. Several Warrens were mayors of Dover. Waterloo Crescent dates from the 1830s. The picture is a fine study of Victorian costume. Note the elegant carriage outside what is now the Churchill Hotel, the bathing machines near East Cliff, to the right, and the ruinous state of the ancient church of St Mary-in-the-Castle.

Contents

This fine picture from the archives of the *Dover Express* gives us a view from underneath the old Guild-hall which stood on pillars in the Market Square with a butter market below until it was demolished by the Town Council in 1861. On the left is the corner of Igglesden & Grave's bakers, established in 1788. The white-fronted building in Castle Street is Stembrook Mill, on the site of which a supermarket was later built.

Acknowledgements

This book has been compiled from my personal photographic collection and information archive, together with considerable help from the records and newspaper files of the *Dover Express*. I have to acknowledge the generous help over the years of friends such as fellow enthusiasts Joe Harman, Harold Sneller and former Dover Public Library reference librarian Mrs Sylvia Corrall. My thanks also go to the many people who have permitted me to make copies of their precious postcards and family pictures over a period of more than thirty years. I owe a particular debt to the *Dover Express* and its late editor John Bavington Jones for having kept such important original pictures, glass plate negatives, local history information, and copies of local newspapers in addition to those of the *Dover Express* itself. I am also endebted to the staff of the *Dover Express* who over the years have cared for those records and who helped to save them when the old printing works in Snargate Street were badly damaged by fire years ago. I am sorry that I cannot name them all individually. Most of all I thank my wife Kathleen for her considerable input into this book, for her forbearance, her practical help checking text and her wise advice.

Introduction

Dover has been a port for well over 2,000 years and can truly claim to be the 'Gateway to Europe'. Ideally situated for a settlement within reach of Europe, it sits in the valley of the River Dour. The recent find of a unique Bronze Age boat confirmed that ships traversed the Dover Strait, trading or invading, as far back as prehistoric times. Many centuries later hot air balloons and early aircraft succeeded in crossing, heralding a new era of travel. Now we have not only a continuous succession of ferries crossing the Channel every day, carrying millions of passengers a year, but a Channel Tunnel railway link.

Ancient Britons massed and forced the Romans to sail on to Walmer to make their first invasion attempts. The Romans built a fort at Dover to defend their new territory but later left Britain. The Normans, arriving in 1066, restored some stability. By the time of the *Domesday Book*, the Kent section of which was started at Dover, the town had grown to such a size it could provide 400 seamen to man warships. In the sixteenth and seventeenth centuries large numbers of Huguenot refugees fleeing religious persecution came into East Kent, bringing skills and trades and much money, intermarrying into existing communities around Dover.

Commanding the shortest sea route to France has given the town an advantage over other rival ports, and it has had what could be called a cosmopolitan community for a long time. Dover has witnessed a remarkable cavalcade of historic comings and goings. Not least of the distinguished visitors were Queen Elizabeth I and King Henry VIII. Queen Elizabeth made her spectacular tour of Kent in 1573, arriving at Dover via Folkestone, Capel, the Western Heights and Cowgate, into Queen Street, with an escort of a thousand wagons and thousands of followers on horseback travelling over rough tracks. There has been a long succession of notable visitors down the centuries, with hundreds of 'royals', some of them heading for the crusades, and leading statesmen from around the world. For centuries pilgrims to Canterbury, refugees, traders and tourists have been attracted to Dover. In more recent times they have been followed by hundreds of would-be Channel swimmers drawn by this unique challenge. Inevitably, like any seafaring community, Dover has also had tragedies, a succession of wars and threats of invasion, many losses of ships and mariners, as well as other fatalities.

For centuries, wagons, walking, riding or sailing were the only means of travel to other places. Wagons gradually gave way to coaches and horses on rutted tracks. The old Folkestone 'road' that Queen Elizabeth rode, was such a track. A continuation of Limekiln Street, it was turned into a turnpike in 1763. This was later abandoned in favour of an easier, more sheltered route down the valley from Capel via Farthingloe. Now a new A20 follows the old route. On the other side of town, travellers entered Dover via narrow Dolphin Lane and Stembrook, and later, St James Street. It was 1837 before Castle Street gave better access into the Market Square.

It is said civilization and invention go hand in hand and Dover has witnessed many important innovations in aviation, building, ships, and road transport, not to mention wireless telegraphy, radio and radar. Travel vastly improved with the coming of railways but company rivalry delayed their arrival at Dover. The first line reached Folkestone in 1843, but engineers had to blast and tunnel through cliffs, including the Round Down, Shakespeare Cliff and Archcliffe, before reaching Dover in January 1844.

The Dover Corporation Tramway, opened in 1897, was a boon to the working class providing cheap fares and easily undercutting the horse-drawn buses which operated the only other form of public transport. A leader in its time, the tramway was the first council-run system in the south of England. In the first year it carried over 1.75 million passengers between Buckland and the docks, but tram profits were raided to reduce council rates, and inadequate sums were invested in track and cars, so that the system became run down. Trams were a familiar sight in Dover until the end of 1936 when buses took over.

Dover has an important place in English history as one of the Cinque Ports legalized by charter in 1278 and for years was liable to supply ships and men for the Navy. But its strategic position has made it vulnerable, and it has had more than its share of England's invaders and immigrants.

Many Dover businesses have faded or disappeared altogether. The collieries have closed and there has been a big cut-back in the number of troops based here. Local businesses have suffered as a result and small shops in particular have been hit by competition from superstores. But tourism in this White Cliffs Country is expanding and taking over some of the lost employment. It has been boosted by the port aggressively facing up to the challenge of the Channel Tunnel with its modern car ferries and fast craft, and by promoting the cruise liner trade to draw yet more tourists. HM Customs and Excise also continues to provide countless local people with work.

During the Second World War, bombing and relentless shelling by big guns installed by the Germans on the French coast changed the character of Dover for ever. Nearly a thousand homes and commercial buildings were destroyed and nearly three thousand severely damaged, earning Dover the nickname of 'Hellfire Corner'. Thankfully, we still have some attractive and historic buildings, including the castle, the Roman pharos, St Mary-in-the-Castle and other churches such as St Mary's and St Andrew's, and St Edmund's Chapel. There is the Roman Painted House (of AD 200), a medieval Maison Dieu with magnificent stained glass windows of the 1870s, the adjoining Maison Dieu House and looking out to sea across Marine Parade, a fine crescent which includes Churchill's Hotel.

Adding to the attractions are the two water-mills, one in the main street and the other at River, Kearsney Abbey parkland, Connaught Park and Pencester Gardens, Shakespeare Cliff (described in Shakespeare's *King Lear*), Langdon Cliffs and the Napoleonic fortifications on the Western Heights. Modern assets include The White Cliffs Experience, Samphire Hoe nature reserve and a yacht marina. Watching over them all, a number of amenity groups help provide a strong and influential public voice, working to enhance the district and helping to boost tourism. Long may it continue!

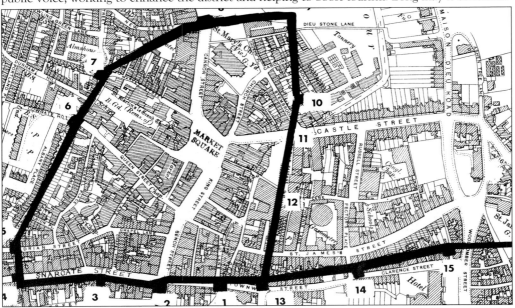

The old town walls and their gates or towers superimposed on a street map of the early 1900s. 1. Butchery Gate or Standfast Tower, removed in 1819; 2. Severus Gate, removed c. 1762; 3. Snar Gate, a tower in Wellington Passage; 4. Snargate, built in 1370 further down Snargate Street, demolished in 1683; 5. Adrian Gate, or Upwall Gate; 6. Cow Gate, Queen Street, demolished in 1776; 7. St Martin's or Monk's Gate; 8. Biggin Gate, taken down in 1762; 9. No name, Dieu Stone Lane; 10. Tinker's Tower, Stembrook; 11. No name, Castle Street; 12. Dolphin Lane, an ancient entrance to the walled town; 13. Fisher's Gate at the sea-shore, shown on old maps and sketches. Some of these towers were used as prisons.

One

Landmarks and General Views

Dover Castle, seen here around 1890, is one of the best-preserved and most attractively sited Norman castles in Europe. In 1216 Hubert de Burgh, with 140 men, successfully defended it against the Dauphin of France. Beneath the fortress are Napoleonic and Second World War tunnels and underground operation rooms, many of which are now open to the public. There was also a secret regional seat of government created here during the cold war. For years it has been one of the United Kingdom's top ten tourist attractions. In recent years the castle has been managed by English Heritage which has carried out improvements and opened up the view of the castle by felling many trees which covered the attractive hillside and ramparts. Special events, including exhibitions and re-enactments of ancient battles, help to draw more and more visitors. This view by Martin Jacolette is from the top of Connaught Park, opened in 1883 by the Duke and Duchess of Connaught. The photographer's pony and trap are concealed by the shrubs growing around the small, ornate, park entrance gate.

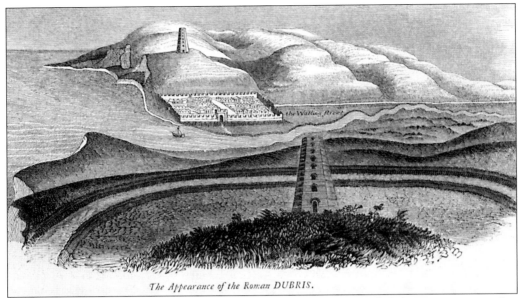

The Appearance of the Roman DUBRIS.

A nineteenth-century engraving depicts a pair of Roman pharos, or lighthouses, one on either side of the Heights. They are said to have guided Roman galleys across the Straits to Dover. The only surviving pharos stands next to St Mary-in-the-Castle. Once up to 80ft high it looked down on a walled Roman town, on the western side of the Dour valley, which has been excavated in recent times. For years the colourful ceremony to install a new Lord Warden of the Cinque Ports was held at the western pharos site.

The 350ft high rock-face of Shakespeare Cliff with newly-cut hay on the upper slopes of Aycliffe, photographed by Jacolette around 1890. Deeds belonging to Aycliffe Farm, which owned the land at the top of the cliff, are said to refer to Shakespeare Cliff, once known as the Great Archcliffe, by its old name of Hay Cliff. Now the new A20 trunk-road has been driven through this area, and can hardly be said to enhance the national landmark so beloved of Shakespeare who described it in *King Lear*.

10

A view of Dover from the Priory Field: this 1807 engraving shows the Maison Dieu to the left of centre, behind the harvesters, and the ancient Dover Priory through the trees on the right. The priory once occupied a large area at the corner of Folkestone Road and the main street. The print dates back a century before John Bavington Jones, editor of the *Dover Express* from 1873 to 1922, used it as the frontispiece to his book *Dover – A Perambulation of the Town, Port and Fortress*, published in 1907.

The Cause is Altered, one of the oldest inns in town, stood at the top of Queen Street, at the junction with Princes Street, and was swept away to build the York Street dual carriageway in 1972. How the old Black Horse came to be called the Cause is Altered is disputed, but innkeeper M.A. Bourn is said to have shunned its links with smuggling, thus changing the 'cause'. A plaque on the pub corner marked the site of Cow Gate in the town wall, which stood there until 1776. The bicycle belonged to Joe Harman, a retired ambulance officer, who took this photograph.

Dover town centre is the backdrop to this pastoral scene, painted from within the grounds of the old Dover Priory Farm complete with its monastic fish-ponds, off Effingham Crescent. The Maison Dieu, now the town hall, is on the far left. The ponds could be where the monks bred fish for food. In contrast during the 1900s as the site of Dover College this was the scene of numerous ceremonies to install a new Lord Warden.

Dover College gateway, seen here around 1860, is one of three main relics of the original Dover Priory of St Martin. The others are the refectory and the old guest-house, later used as a farmhouse and now as a chapel. In 1871 the derelict priory, long used as a farm, was adapted for use by Dover College which today is a coeducational prep school. Several college buildings were damaged during the Second World War but were subsequently restored.

The Burlington Hotel, viewed here from the Promenade Pier around 1890, stood on a site which in more recent years was long occupied by a filling-station on the corner of Townwall Street and Woolcomber Street, since also demolished. It was first called the Clarence Hotel and was built in the 1860s on the site of Clarence House, the home of the Rice banking family. Edward Royds Rice was Liberal MP for Dover for twenty years. Later turned into flats, the Burlington Hotel was devastated in the Second World War and demolished in 1949.

Victoria Park, a fine crescent nestling below Dover Castle, dates from 1864 and stands on what was known as Stringer's Field, named after landowner Phineas Stringer. These houses, with polished mahogany staircases and, at one time, croquet lawns, were built for families of means, some having up to nine servants. More recently these houses have become flats. It is said that Winston Churchill once stayed here during the Second World War, No. 21 reputedly having blast-proof walls.

Maison Dieu House in Biggin Street, pictured here between the wars, is now the public library. Built in 1665 for the Agent Victualler of the Maison Dieu victualling yard, it is said to be the house alluded to in Ingoldsby's *Old Woman in Grey* while an associated bakery (later W. Burkett's) was close by in Biggin Street. In front of Maison Dieu House is Dover war memorial unveiled in 1924 by Sir Roger Keyes and now honouring the dead of two world wars.

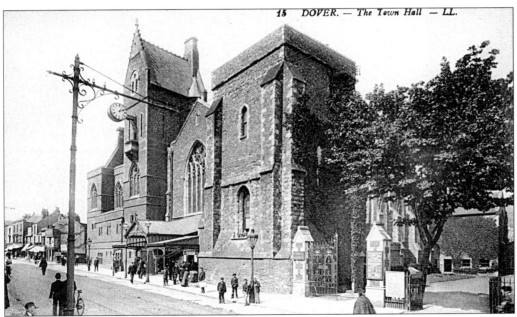

The Maison Dieu, for many years the town hall, pictured around 1910. This view dates from the days of Dover tramways, the overhead power lines being suspended from the post on the left which stood at the Biggin Street junction with Effingham Crescent. Note the gates at the entrance to Maison Dieu House on the right and the ornate canopy over the town hall steps.

Two

Streets, Trade and Industry

Ashen Tree Lane was part of an area once known as Tinker's Close where there used to be a market, called the Upmarket, from as early as 1430. Both buildings, viewed from Castle Hill around 1850, survive. White-fronted and with a knapped flint finish, Ashen Tree House has a 1641 date plaque and is much altered. It adjoined a dairy, reputed in 1899 to date back 200 years. Cows were kept behind the property on the right. The old sign reads: 'Milk and cream sold by Widow Baker, daughter of the late Widow Clara'.

Mr and Mrs George Briggs stand in the doorway of their general shop in Trevanion Street around 1883. The Dover Sports Centre now stands here. Trevanion Street ran from St James' church to the sea and was named after John Trevanion, MP for Dover from 1774 to 1806. This MP had a mansion and farm below the cliff, in an area that was badly damaged in the Second World War and later cleared of homes and shops. Henshaw Latham of the Dover Gaslight Co. opened the first gasworks to light the streets here in 1822.

Pencester Road at its junction with Biggin Street, c. 1910. Hookway's outfitters traded here from the mid-1890s, later moving to premises a few doors nearer to St Mary's church. From around 1914 the firm of Murdoch's traded here in musical instruments and electrical goods for about fifty years. Rooms above what later became a record shop have been occupied by the Oddfellows' Club and Institute since 1885.

The Market Square, around 1947 looking up Castle Street with Igglesden & Grave's the bakers (established in 1788) on one corner and Flashman's furniture shop on the other. On the right is the old Phoenix Brewery. This picture was taken after the clearance of war damaged property. In 1905 Igglesden's was rebuilt with a Tudor style frontage, and Lloyds Bank was built next door. Charles Dickens placed his character David Copperfield on Igglesden's steps searching for his Aunt Betsey Trotwood.

King Street looking towards the Market Square and Church Street, c. 1890. This photograph of a shoeblack and carts in the Market Square area paints a picture of a vastly different age to that of today. The picture is from a collection of old hand-tinted magic lantern slides. Slideshows were very popular more than a century ago before the advent of the cinema.

A row of old flint cottages on London Road, two of them called Pear Tree Cottages, stood on the water-mill side of the junction with Cherry Tree Avenue until the early 1970s. They should have been preserved along with most of the property on the same side of the road as far as Buckland Bridge. So much of the character of the old town has been lost through the demolition of interesting buildings.

Snargate Street in the early 1930s, before wartime devastation changed this important shopping area forever. Children walk fearlessly in the centre of the narrow street outside what became Worrall's café and the Trocadero bars, wine store and lounge, on the corner of Five Post Lane. Barely visible is one of a series of distinctive street lights which were suspended from ornamental arches across the street, starting at the offices of the *Dover Express*.

Snargate Street in May 1930, when some of the seaward side of the street, along with most of Northampton Street, was being demolished in a Commercial Quay improvement. In the centre is Snargate Street Methodist Chapel, next to the Grand Shaft, a unique triple stairway through the cliff to the barracks above. Barracks and church have gone but the staircase remains as a tourist attraction. Close by was the laundry of Scott & Sons, a century old in 1952, and the Mitre public house, sandwiched between two garages.

Snargate Street, close to the junction with New Bridge and Northampton Street, in the 1970s. On the left is Worrall's café and next door to it Weir's the chemists, formerly Igglesden's jewellers. Outside was a public clock, now in Deal. At the side of Weir's was Chapel Street, leading to Adrian Street and the Unitarian church. All of these old properties shown, except for Hart's shop at the Bench Street corner (in recent years an amusement arcade), came down to build the York Street dual carriageway and a roundabout.

The junction of Castle Street and the Market Square in 1929, when the Granada Cinema was being built on the Phoenix Brewery yard. On the right is Flashman's furniture showroom, later replaced by a modern store. Contractors are moving a long girder around Igglesden & Grave's bakery corner to the cinema site. Hubbard's umbrella shop at No. 81, on the left, and the adjoining Pickford's offices were blasted by the last shell to hit Dover in the Second World War.

Castle Street close to the junction with Russell Street in the late 1920s. There is a variety of shops, cafés, tobacconist's and confectioner's, solicitors, an electrician's, and a large brewery. Dover's first super-cinema, the Granada/ABC, was built on the site of the brewery yard. The cinema, which could seat 1,700 people, was later converted to a night-club.

Charlton Green post office in Maison Dieu Road, near Peter Street, before road widening and the building of a new sub post office and adjoining Grapes public house. A placard outside Mr R. Grey's post office and newsagent's shop, announcing the shelling of Taku forts in the Boxer Rebellion in China, dates the picture to 1900. Near this site, now dominated by a B&Q store, once stood Palmerstone Terrace, the Sportsman Inn, Cook's Cottages and Castle Cottages.

Narrow Worthington's Lane was widened during these street improvements in 1894-1895, earning its new name, Worthington Street. Previously an ancient narrow track called Gardiner's Lane, it became Worthington's Lane about 1800 when the Worthington family owned property here. They also owned the Ship Hotel on Custom House Quay, at the Granville Dock, wine-vaults in the Snargate Street cliffs, behind the present Masonic Hall (once the London and County Bank), and a mansion and later a brewery at Maxton.

Ladywell at the turn of the twentieth century. In 1867 the street, cobbled and only 14ft wide, was virtually the boundary between town and open fields. In 1900 it was widened to 20ft and two houses were converted into the Sir John Falstaff public house. Ten years later, after this picture was taken, the Sir John Falstaff was rebuilt nearer the main street. This colourful pub, with its attractive tiled frontage, was extensively renovated in 1981.

Ladywell and Park Street, looking towards the High Street, during a procession of Friendly Society members in the 1920s. On the corner of Dour Street, a road leading off to the right by the tree, was A.S. Wootton, the grocer's, while Jude Hanbury & Co. Canterbury ales and stout were being sold at the Sir John Falstaff public house and advertised on its end wall. Ladywell is named after a public well which once stood at the rear of the Maison Dieu.

St James' Street, to the left, was once on the main coaching route to Deal from Dover before Castle Street was built up to the Market Square. This photograph was taken looking down St James' Lane around 1890. On the right, just beyond Sedgewick's second-hand furniture shop, is the weather-boarded Town Mill which survived until after the Second World War. Under the lamp was F. Chatwin, the naturalist's pet shop.

Adrian Street ran parallel with Snargate Street from behind the old *Dover Express* printing-works to the allotments and Cowgate Cemetery on the slopes of the Western Heights. Pictured in April 1937, the old stone and flint house on the right is boarded up prior to the demolition of all properties on that side for road widening and building new homes. Close by stands the former Baptist church, now Adrian Street Unitarian church.

Joseph Carter's cobblers shop on the corner of Stembrook and Church Street. Stembrook sloped down from Castle Street, past Stembrook water-mill, to a ford across the River Dour. Church Street, to the right, led to the Market Square past the old Star Inn, where local celebrity the 'Fat Man of Dover' Thomas Longley was licensee. He was once the United Kingdom's heaviest man, weighing 42 stone. In the background, in Castle Street, are the former offices of Leney's Phoenix Brewery.

Tranquil Limekiln Street in late 1935. A re-routed A20 trunk-road now runs through this street from Shakespeare Cliff and the area known loosely as Aycliffe or Archcliffe to the Eastern Docks. There it meets a second London Road, the A2, at the foot of Jubilee Way. Most of the property shown, including a block of council flats, was demolished to build the new dual carriageway which replaces the old A20 route via Folkestone Road, now the B2011.

Middle Row, between Council House Street and Beach Street, with Alfred Virgo's grocers shop, is typical of a heavily populated area once known as The Pier. This district was bordered by Lord Warden Square, Shakespeare Beach, Archcliffe Fort, Limekiln Street, at the foot of the cliffs below the Western Heights, Granville Dock and Clarence Place. At the corner of the street opposite the shop was the chapel of St John Mariners' church. This photograph, taken around 1910, is by Amos & Amos.

One of the timber-framed buildings which used to line Snargate Street. Possibly dating back to the sixteenth century, in later times buildings such as this would have had new frontages built of brick added on to them. Many properties in the town, in the main street for instance, may be found to have once been timber framed and fronted. This drawing by Thomas Hastings dates from between 1821-1824, and is part of the Lord Astor of Hever Collection which was presented to Dover Museum in 1963 by Mr R.B. Dunwoody.

One of the oldest buildings in town, dating from 1203, the Maison Dieu was a pilgrims' hospital for 330 years followed by 300 years as a Navy victualling office. Now the town hall, it once housed the old town prison. Most of the prison was demolished to build the fine Connaught Hall, opened in 1883 by the Duke and Duchess of Connaught. Until 1987 magistrates' and coroner's courts sat here in what was once a medieval chapel.

Houses such as this one on Beach Street, backing onto the railway at the top of Shakespeare Beach, were quite common in years gone by. Part flint, part timber, they were demolished because they were considered to be little better than hovels. This cottage, at the western end of the street, was photographed by Amos & Amos in a series dating from around 1912, a time of great change and new building, including new council houses at Beach Street built around 1913-1916.

Shipdem's House, or the Round House, faced Granville Gardens and backed onto Townwall Street. Demolished after Second World War shelling, this Regency villa was built for John Shipdem, Town Clerk and Register of Dover harbour from 1791. It was said he built it round so that the devil couldn't catch him in a corner! In 1835 he breakfasted at the Ship Hotel with Princess Victoria and her mother the Duchess of Kent. Later the Round House was a British Legion club.

At barely 12ft wide, Worthington's Lane, now Worthington Street, had only enough room for a horse and cart. This is the Biggin Street junction just before Charles Wood's butchers shop on the left was taken down to widen Worthington's Lane. The butcher switched to new premises on the opposite corner where the old Central Bakery, formerly Holmes Morris, had been pulled down. Later Timothy White's took it over and for years Boots the Chemists was on the opposite corner. Holmes Morris moved over the road.

The Odeon Cinema, London Road, was originally known as the Regent Cinema which was opened on 27 March 1937 by the Lord Warden, the Marquess of Willingdon, for its owners Universal Cinema Theatres Ltd. The Regent Cinema was built on a site adjoining the Buckland Picture Palace, which closed on 31 May 1936. The new cinema had seating for 1,850 for stage and film shows, and in July 1943 it became the Odeon Cinema. Closure came on 2 October 1971 and a TA training centre was built in its place.

The Royal Hippodrome, a wartime favourite, stood on the site of an earlier theatre, the Clarence, which had been there at least as far back as 1790. Rebuilt as the Tivoli Theatre it opened in June 1897, Queen Victoria's Diamond Jubilee year. It later became the Theatre Royal, and was sold in 1899 to a Ramsgate buyer for £6,300. In the early 1900s it was renamed the Royal Hippodrome. Many famous artistes and strippers trod the boards here, but in September 1944 the theatre was destroyed by one of the last enemy shells to hit Dover.

Although the Empire in the Market Square laid claim in 1909 to being the town's first cinema, the upper floors of the Apollonian public house in Snargate Street had been converted into a People's Picture Palace even before that date. Posters in the windows at the pub entrance advertise 'Sanger's Animated Pictures'. Nearby, the Wellington Hall in Snargate Street was showing 'Shanly's Electric Animated Pictures' in 1911. The Apollonian was demolished in the 1930s.

The Granada Cinema with nearly 1,700 seats was billed as the 'Granada Luxury Theatre', and had a Russian designer commissioned by Sidney, later Lord, Bernstein. The Castle Street 'palace' was built on the brewer's yard of Alfred Leney. Huge stone blocks had to be laid in the bed of the River Dour as anchors for metal girders, and work barely finished in time for the opening on 8 January 1930. Called the ABC Cinema from 1960, it closed in October 1982 and became a night-club.

The White Horse Inn on St James' Street, next to the old St James' church, around 1930 when it was owned by brewers George Beer & Co. Probably the oldest public house in town, a former landlord said it was built in 1365 and from 1574 was occupied by the town's 'ale taster', the forerunner of later weights and measures inspectors. In 1652 Nicholas Ramsey obtained a licence to sell ales and cider next to the church. From 1635 known as the City of Edinburgh, the White Horse took its present name in 1818.

The Hotel de France and Café de Paris at New Bridge, March 1967. It was once the King's Arms Library and meeting rooms, owned by William Batcheller, the publisher of the *Dover Telegraph* which ran from November 1833 until 1927. He also produced pocket guides including *A New History of Dover and Dover Castle* published in 1828. Later editions had fine woodcut engravings of principal Dover features. Batcheller's Library later became Cuff's Library, then, after the Second World War, a hotel and restaurant. It was demolished around 1971.

Dover Colliery before 1910. The colliery was built on land created by blowing up Round Down Cliff to construct the railway between Dover and Folkestone. Here the Kent coalfield began, with four collieries eventually creating 7,000 jobs. Coal was found in 1890 by drilling shafts on an abandoned Channel tunnel site. Intolerable flooding and loss of life at Dover Colliery forced its closure by 1915 after only little coal was raised, and this is now the site of the Samphire Hoe nature reserve.

Dover fish market in the Council House Street area during the South Eastern & Chatham Railway period. This district used to be known as The Pier. When the Dover tramway service opened in 1897 the level-crossing shown had to be traversed by tramcars to reach the Clarence Place terminus in the background. Because of delays caused by the frequent closing of the crossing gates, trams ceased running further than the Crosswall Quay stop after April 1898.

Dawes' Diamond Brewery, Maxton, viewed from the lower slopes of Stebbing Down or Plum Pudding Hill around 1894. This photograph by Whorwell, of Bench Street, appeared in the *Dover Standard* on 29 August 1894. The old A20 Folkestone Road runs across the foot of the picture hidden by a hedge. The brewery was once owned by one of the Worthington family of hoteliers and coach proprietors. The large building on the left, now demolished, is Maxton Manor.

Buckland Paper Mill around 1880 viewed across the churchyard of St Andrew's church, with its famous yew tree. This ancient yew, well over 1,000 years old, still flourishes after a remarkable move in 1880 to make room for a big extension to the church. Critics said it would kill the tree, but expert William Barron and his men from Derby moved the 56 ton mass 60ft to the west.

Dover Engineering Works foundry, *c.* 1973. This foundry at the corner of Charlton Green and Bridge Street celebrated its centenary in 1930, and was a major employer for decades. It made gastight manhole covers of all kinds, exporting all over the world. These were patented by Vivian Elkington, who took over from A.L. Thomas & Sons, and bear his name. The foundry closed in the late 1980s, some years after Mr Elkington died, and a B&Q store was built on the site.

Chitty's Mill, Granville Street, once one of the town's biggest businesses, seen here between the wars. Shire-horses stand patiently as carts are loaded with flour. This photograph came from the Osborne and Smith families, three generations of whom worked at the mill. Horses worked alongside Foden steam-wagons. A water-tower made the mill a target for enemy guns during the Second World War and it was so badly damaged that demolition soon followed. Now Halfords stands on the site.

New Bridge with the timber yard of Steriker Finnis & Sons in the foreground, cleared to build Cambridge Terrace in 1856. Behind the yard to the left is Batcheller's Library, later the Hotel de France, which also came down for road building (see page 30). William Batcheller, who built his library in 1826, founded the *Dover Telegraph* newspaper (1833-1936). New Bridge has been sliced through by the Townwall Street dual carriageway, part of the new A20 to Folkestone.

Buckland Paper Mill at the foot of Crabble Hill around 1920, with Dover Corporation Tramways car No. 15 or 16 passing after a run to River. Then owned by Wiggins Teape the Dover mill business dates from 1770. The clock tower dates from around 1888-1895. Sadly, in 1999 came the news that the mill was to close the following year, a major blow to Dover industry. On the right stood a row of cottages demolished just before the Second World War and later the site of a petrol filling station. Efforts have been made to save the clocktower.

The Market Square in the 1970s with the market hall (now the site of Dover Museum) and Warren & Reynold's wholesale grocers warehouse behind it (later the White Cliffs Experience). The business, formerly Richard Dickeson & Co., was established in 1649 and had a number of branches. Proprietor from 1665 was Dover Baptist leader Samuel Tavener who died in 1696. He was formerly a captain of horse under Oliver Cromwell. One-time owner Sir Richard Dickeson was mayor of Dover four times between 1871 and 1882.

The Windmill Brewery during its clearance in July 1983, including, on the right at the back of the site, the square, weather-boarded base, with tiled roof, of the former windmill. The windmill pumped pure water from a deep well to be used for brewing beer. Surviving a few streets away is an old malt-house which probably supplied the malt. For years the brewery buildings housed the coach works of George Sacre Palmer, his son Walter, and then Jenkins & Pain.

Dover Gasworks in May 1955, looking across Coombe Valley Road to Green Lane and Mayfield Avenue. The works, established in 1864, spanned the valley from gasholders and storage tanks on one side, to a massive retort house, and coal and coke yards on the other. Coombe Valley Road runs diagonally across from the prefabs in the foreground on the left to the former George Palmer coach works at the bottom of the road on the right.

A nineteenth-century water-colour of the Windmill Brewery, London Road. The painting belonged to the late Lt-Col. James Kingsford Carson, a descendant of the brewery owner Alfred Kingsford. Mr Carson presented a copy of the picture to residents of Kingsford Court when he performed the official opening ceremony there on 24 October 1989. The flats were built on the brewery site.

The *Peter Hawksfield*, a collier named after a master mariner who built up a fleet of three cargo sailing-ships at Dover and, in 1876, founded P. Hawksfield & Son Ltd, in St James' Street. He ran a growing business bringing coal to the port and selling it. Three generations of the family expanded the business, acquiring other firms around the coast. The family name was retained until 1962 when it became Corrall Ltd, with brothers Kenneth and Peter Hawksfield as leading directors.

Three
Church and School

SS Peter & Paul church, Charlton, built in 1893, and beside it the old building by the River Dour it was to replace. The previous church had been rebuilt in 1827 on the foundations of an older building, a church having stood at Charlton Green from at least 1291. This charming old church was too small for a growing parish, and instead of being retained for use as a chapel or church hall, it was demolished in the same year that the new church was built.

St Mary's parish church, Cannon Street, *c.* 1900. St Mary's is listed in the *Domesday Book* and part of the church is said to stand on the remains of a Roman bath. Retaining attractive columns supporting two rows of arches, it was extensively rebuilt in 1843 but the tower dates from 1100. Note the overhead tram wires and double tram tracks in Cannon Street. On the left is the Wellington public house which was demolished to build a supermarket.

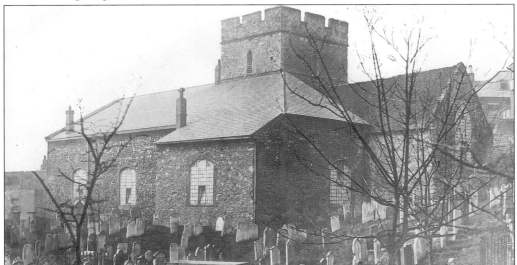

Old St James' church, *c.* 1865. The fabric of St James' was largely of Norman origin. In 1635 the sea came up to the building and later there was an old harbour close by. Cinque Ports' Courts of Admiralty were held in the church until 1863 and the Lord Warden had a chapel there. Extensively restored in the 1860s and renovated again in the 1930s, the church was devastated by enemy action in the Second World War. The collapse of the tower ended hopes of repair but it is maintained as a tidy ruin.

Buckland School, London Road, c. 1965. The school opened in 1859 and although the building survives it is no longer a school. The end came in 1966-67. A campaign to save the school failed and pupils were transferred to Barton Road School. A feature is the distinctive clocktower and bell. The bell came from the sailing-ship the *Earl of Eglinton* which was wrecked in St Margaret's Bay in 1860. The weather-vane displays the date 1879. Sadly the old clock has gone but the bell is preserved in nearby St Andrew's church, Buckland.

Salem Baptist Chapel and Schools in Biggin Street with an appeal for subscriptions to raise £3,000 to build a new Sunday school at the rear of the chapel. The chapel was demolished, along with the attractive Queen's Head public house adjoining, to build a larger Boots the Chemists in the early 1970s. A new Baptist church was built in Maison Dieu Road, near the Five Ways junction.

St Andrew's church, Buckland, pictured soon after the completion of an extension which required the removal of an adjoining ancient yew tree to a new position some 60ft to the west in 1880. The move was completely successful and the tree flourished. The *Domesday Book* lists a church at Buckland. Around 1196 the monks of Dover Priory built a church in place of an earlier Saxon building on their lands at Buckland, and the older columns and arches in St Andrew's are their work.

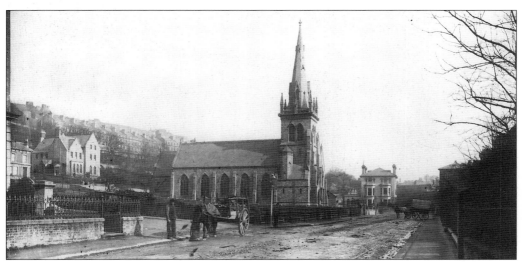

New St James' church, Maison Dieu Road, pictured soon after its construction around 1890. Victoria Park can be seen in the background. It was called 'new' to distinguish it from the ancient church of the same name. The church was demolished after the Second World War during which it had been only slightly damaged. With a reduced congregation it was judged to be redundant, like several other parish churches, and was demolished.

The church of St Mary-in-the-Castle adjoins a Roman pharos, or lighthouse, and is believed to pre-date the Norman Conquest. The oldest Anglican church in regular use for services, it has Saxon chancel walls and two Saxon double-splayed windows each side of the nave. The church was once joined to the Roman lighthouse, which served as a bell-tower. There has been a church here since AD 180. It lost its roof and came close to being demolished but in 1857 the government announced it would be saved. St Mary-in-the-Castle was extensively restored in the latter part of the nineteenth century.

St Edmund's long-forgotten thirteenth-century wayside chapel was hemmed in by property on Biggin Street and Priory Road. It became a whitesmith's forge, as pictured in this 1939 drawing by Mabel Martin, and later a Toc H charity workshop. Consecrated by Richard, Bishop of Chichester, in AD 1253, the chapel was saved from demolition in 1966 by Catholic priest Fr Terence Tanner who raised money to buy and restore it. On 27 May 1968 it was re-consecrated by the Rt Revd Cyril Cowderoy, Archbishop of Southwark.

Holy Trinity church, seen here around 1850, stood close to the railway line from Folkestone which went through the old Harbour Station and a tunnel under the Heights to Dover Priory Station. The church served a large seafaring community known as The Pier, but after slum clearance, before and after the Second World War, it became redundant and was demolished. From the Shipwright's Arms and Packet Boat Inn, on the left, Union Safe stage-coaches left twice daily for the White Bear Inn, Piccadilly, the Bell & Crown, Holborn, or Blossom's Inn on Cheapside. Fortunately the original 10 inch by 12 inch glass negative of this photograph, rescued from an office fire, survives.

Above: St Mary's Church of England Girls' School, Princes Street, *c.* 1900. The boys' school was around the corner in Queen Street. Next door to the school stands a gateway which once led to the churchyard and massive church of St Martin le Grand in the Market Square. The poet Charles Churchill, and Baptist leader, Samuel Tavener were both buried here. Tavener, who had been a Captain under Cromwell, died in 1696. The churchyard, schools and adjoining Cause is Altered public house were all cleared to build the York Street dual carriageway.

Right: St James' Street was once on the main coaching route to Deal from Dover. In the centre, on the right-hand side, is the former Gordon Boys' Orphanage founded by Thomas Blackman. Most of this narrow street has been demolished as a result of war damage and replaced by a car park. On the left stood the old Red Lion public house and the St James' Church of England primary school (centre).

St Radigund's twelfth-century abbey, not far from the Dover town boundary, on the route from St Radigund's Road to West Hougham. This gateway was the tower of the ruined abbey church, while the building behind it, used as a farmhouse for centuries, was the refectory. The first abbot was Hugh who probably watched over the abbey's construction towards the end of the twelfth century. In the fifteenth century allegations of corruption were levelled at the monks who were then evicted. Now the site is farmed.

Dover Priory around 1870 showing, on the left, the tunnel through which the London, Chatham & Dover Railway brought their line to Priory Station in 1861. At this time there were no houses on top of Priory Hill looking down on the priory buildings and the future site of Dover College. To the right of centre is the priory gateway which appears elsewhere in this book (on page 12). Beyond the gateway smoke rises from what is now the college chapel but was then a farmhouse.

Four
Around the Harbour

Wellington Dock slipway features in many early port photographs of around 1850, the year the slipway was built, when photographs has barely been invented. On the right is part of Gun Wharf where an ancient crane, which is preserved, was used to raise and lower guns and gun barrels into and out of sailing-ships. It seems sad that the slipway should have been cleared, now the dock is a marina. The town has discarded so many historic links with its past.

Dover harbour, castle and Cinque Ports ships from an original Cottonian manuscript, over 6ft long, in the British Museum which dates from around 1543. This Victorian copy is in the *Dover Express* archives and, although somewhat crude, records a great deal of information about the early port. On the left is the Paradise Harbour that John Clerk helped to form in 1495. From this harbour King Henry VIII embarked for the Field of the Cloth of Gold in 1520. The drawing also shows Dover's churches, town wall and gates.

The Wellington Dock around 1904 during the building of the Admiralty Pier extension, begun in 1899. The *Empress*, with twin funnels, and the *Dover* are the steamers alongside Union Street Quay, both dwarfing an older ship near the Wellington Dock swing bridge. The bridge was widened soon afterwards to allow for bigger steamers, and strengthened to carry express boat-trains serving Atlantic liners berthing at the end of the Prince of Wales Pier, the nearer of the two piers on the left. The metal rings on Gun Wharf were to line the shafts of Dover Colliery.

The Western Docks, looking across Granville Dock, by R. Sedgefield, c. 1865. Work is under way here to complete the Admiralty Pier, started in 1847, which can be seen in the centre extending out to sea. Later a turret was built at the end to house two 81 ton defence guns, which are still there. The Granville Dock was drained in 1871 to deepen it for larger steamers and the clock and compass towers were built. On the extreme right is Holy Trinity church and Harbour Station, while in the centre, just in front of Admiralty Pier, is the Lord Warden Hotel which was linked to Town Station by an overhead footbridge.

Granville Dock in 1879 with a variety of sailing-ships at Crosswall Quay, Custom House Quay and Commercial Quay, viewed from Union Street Quay. In Strond Street, to the right of the dock, the twin towers of Holy Trinity church blend into the masts of the ships. The Ship Hotel, where Wellington celebrated after the battle of Waterloo in 1815, can be seen on the far side of the dock in between the ships. Union Street, once a busy commercial centre and now the route to the hoverport, is today flanked on either side by yacht basins.

A bird's-eye view of the Western Docks in 1840 from an engraving reproduced in a series of postcards once printed and sold by the *Dover Express*. The *Express* is the last survivor of four weekly newspapers which were running side by side into the 1930s. In the foreground is Wellington Dock, with a bridged link to the Granville Dock through Union Quay at the Northampton Street side. From Granville Dock there was access to the tidal harbour via a further dock gate. There was no Admiralty Pier then.

The Grand Shaft Barracks on the Western Heights look down on Granville Dock and Worthington's Royal Ship Hotel. The basis of an extensive family business, the hotel entertained prominent guests, ran coaches to London, and the family later had a brewery at Maxton and wine-vaults in Snargate Street. On the extreme left is a timber-boarded warehouse of the Dover Hoy Co. The dock was a hive of commercial activity for centuries but is now too small for many cargo ships and has been turned into a yacht marina.

The Western Docks area with Union Street Quay in the foreground viewed from the Western Heights before 1880. Note the old steamers alongside the quay and George Hammond's three and four-storey warehouses. Catamaran steamer the *Calais-Douvres*, with four funnels, has steam up just inside Granville Dock on the right. A Dover Harbour Board tug waits just outside the old Wellington Dock gates to help the steamer, but the Crosswall gates are closed.

An early twentieth-century photograph of Wellington Dock by Amos & Amos shows an extensive range of mainly commercial property on the seaward side. Most prominent was the Esplanade Hotel, on the right behind a sailing ship and opposite the entrance to the Prince of Wales Pier. On the quayside are the pilotage offices and stores of Trinity House, boat builders' yards and huts, and a small crane which has been preserved. Photographer George Amos was in Dover from 1858-1914.

The Western Docks around 1887, with Union Street Quay in the foreground, during the widening of the Wellington Dock entrance to 70ft to take bigger steamers. Alongside Union Street – now the route to the hoverport – is believed to be SS *Foam*, of 1862. Note George Hammond's warehouses and the steamers. Commercial premises in the foreground included the Grand Shaft Stores, Dover Castle Tea Stores, Hill's pastry-cook, and the Duke of Cambridge and Mitre hotels.

Shakespeare Beach and the old pilots' watch-tower around 1902, in front of the old Town Station which adjoined the former Lord Warden Hotel, latterly known as Southern House. On the left is a block yard where massive concrete blocks were stored for building the Admiralty Harbour. On the Western Heights, to the left, is the Citadel, and, centre, the army barracks and forts built to defend the town in the event of an attack by Napoleon's army. Trains once ran through the pilots' watch-tower.

The white cliffs of Dover beyond East Cliff around 1860, from an original 12 by 10 inch glass plate negative which is still held in a local archive. Close examination reveals a network of cliff paths, and caves pressed into use as homes by boatmen of the Burville family of that time. Members of this family are believed to be the tiny figures standing outside the caves, or on the beach below, who can be seen with the aid of a strong magnifying glass. Now reclaimed land in the foreground is occupied by one of the busiest passenger terminals in the world.

Cutting away the cliffs to reclaim land from the sea to build the Admiralty Harbour, photographed on 9 April 1900. Many thousands of tons of chalk were cut away by men suspended from ropes down the cliff, or by massive steam-powered excavators. A considerable area was filled in and a network of railway tracks sped the process of reclamation. Rail wagons cross a timber viaduct over the beach to where the new sea-wall and the Eastern Arm of the harbour are taking shape.

Athol Terrace, East Cliff, set back from the sea front promenade, c. 1880. These properties survived the cliff reclamation work to the east to extend the harbour and build the 3,320ft Eastern Arm. Just beyond the houses a railway track was cut up the cliff face to link with the main Deal line at Martin Mill. Many of these properties were guest-houses offering views contrasting vividly with the hustle of today's ferry terminal.

East Cliff, 12 October 1900. A close-up of a primitive-looking steam-excavator used in the reclamation. Near the top, in the original picture, is what appears to be a cave. Several old Dover fishing families lived in the cliffs before the harbour work began. Families of some of the fourteen workmen in this picture probably live in the Dover area today. On the left an overcoat conceals the photographer's case for his huge 12 by 10 inch glass plate negatives.

East Cliff, looking towards the Promenade Pier, around 1895, before building of the Eastern Arm of the Admiralty Harbour. Work had just started to build the Prince of Wales Pier. This popular amenity, 2,900ft long and costing £600,000, opened in 1902. With its attractive ironwork filled in, it now forms a protective wall for the hoverport, now modified for bigger 'jetfoils'. The open framework was intended to help prevent silting up of the tidal harbour or basin outside the Granville and Wellington docks.

East Cliff block yard, seen here in the autumn of 1901, occupied land reclaimed from the sea. Blocks were made on the spot from materials brought from Richborough via the Martin Mill railway, down a cliff-face track, and also by sea. The blocks, dovetailed and keyed together with columns of concrete, were laid at the rate of 600 a month and the Eastern Arm was completed in 1904. The big harbour was thought to be necessary to protect part of the British fleet from a deadly new invention – the torpedo.

Admiralty Pier seen from Cheeseman's Head. Begun in 1847, the pier was later extended and widened in stages. It is pictured here at the stage it had reached by 1871, but with a turret at the end housing two 81 ton guns. The guns were soon out of date and hardly ever fired. In bad weather steamers would sometimes berth on the outside of the pier. The steamer on the inside is believed to be the *Calais-Douvres II*, said to be the first passenger service steamer to be lit by electricity.

These two photographs of the Southern Breakwater were taken in 1905 by Oliver Bavington Jones, one of the two sons of John Bavington Jones, editor of the *Dover Express*. They show the first blocks appearing above water in January and a massive timber pile, 100ft long and weighing 10 tons, being driven into the sea bed to build a breakwater 90ft high and 55ft wide at its base. The blue gum wood came from Dover in Tasmania. A temporary 'viaduct' bridged the gap between the Eastern Arm and the Breakwater during construction.

Admiralty Pier around 1885, before work began on the £3.5 million Admiralty Harbour. On the outside berth is the Dover to Calais catamaran steamer, *Calais-Douvres*, launched on the Tyne in 1878 and having a speed of only 14.5 knots. It was one of three special vessels designed to spare passengers the dreaded *mal de mer* of travel across the often very choppy Strait of Dover, scene of many storms and graveyard of hundreds of ships.

A Royal Navy squadron viewed from Shakespeare Cliff around 1903. The Eastern Arm appears to be near completion, with the Prince of Wales Pier complete, and the Admiralty Pier extension underway to 4,000ft. The first piles of the Southern Breakwater can be seen. At Shakespeare Beach, on the left, stand 42 ton concrete blocks ready for use. Goliath cranes, on railway tracks, lowered the blocks into place and they were then faced with harder, granite blocks from Derbyshire.

Admiralty Pier photographed by Martin Jacolette around 1890, before extension and widening took place to build the Marine Station. A Stirling mail locomotive is heading an express train for London via Folkestone. The signal-box on the left had storm-shutters to protect the windows in rough weather. Jacolette took many photographs of Dover and had studios at North Brook House in Biggin Street (now the offices of the Halifax Building Society) as well as in London. Jacolette died in 1907.

Admiralty Pier around 1900 with the extension work well underway. The steamer coming in is believed to be the *Leopold II*, built by Denny in 1892, although other suggestions have been the *Princesse Clementine* or *Princesse Henriette*. The other paddle-steamer at the outer berth is said to be a Belgian Marine steamer of the Prins Albert class, dating from 1887. Behind that ship can be seen a temporary lighthouse dwarfing the low-lying original lighthouse further to the east.

Steam locomotive the *Sir William Crundall* was named after a Dover Harbour Board chairman, local timber-merchant, developer and thirteen times mayor of Dover. Mr Crundall managed to persuade the Kaiser to use Dover as a port of call for Atlantic liners in the early twentieth century. The 1910 locomotive was built by Peckett & Sons of Bristol and was driven by Jack Squires. An earlier engine created a stir when transported through the narrow streets and over the River Dour in 1899.

A steam-crane empties skips of chalk brought to the site by train to widen the Admiralty Pier by reclaiming land from the sea to build Marine Station, now a terminal for cruise liners. The date is 9 February 1911. A goods train passes in the shadow of the Lord Warden Hotel, hauled by a South Eastern & Chatham Railway 4-4-0 steam locomotive. This once important hotel later became the headquarters of British Rail for many years, its name becoming Southern House, and in the Second World War it served as naval base HMS Wasp.

Widening Admiralty Pier in 1910 to build the Marine Station, which greatly improved railway facilities for cross-Channel passengers. Heavy seas swept right over the pier, drenching everyone not sheltered by a narrow canopy above the platform. Goliath cranes, of up to 350 tons and with a span of 100ft, lowered pre-formed concrete blocks and outer granite blocks into position, guided by teams of men below. The blocks are stamped with the date they were made – June 1910.

Cranes, and teams of divers operating from small boats, were used during the building of the Train Ferry Dock in 1934. Construction work was delayed once when a crane collapsed and became a mass of twisted metal in the water. The railway signal-box in the foreground was close to Harbour Station. In the background can be seen the Prince of Wales Pier, the Breakwater and, on the right, the end of Admiralty Pier.

Divers inside a diving-bell about 50ft down on the bed of the harbour during the building of the Train Ferry Dock around 1933. Compressed air kept the sea water out as the men worked in shifts lasting up to three hours at a time. The work was hampered considerably by natural springs of fresh water which bubbled up from the sea floor at this point. The initials SP & S are those of S. Pearson & Sons, harbour contractors.

Divers with a large diving-bell, lowered by steam-crane and constantly supplied with air, worked underwater on the foundations of the Train Ferry Dock in the 1930s. Earlier they had helped to construct the harbour walls. Some diving-bells were 17ft long and weighed 30 tons. Divers formed a team eighty strong at the peak of the work in May 1903 when a *Cassell's Magazine* writer 'sampled' the conditions they worked in.

Admiralty Pier and the Train Ferry Dock as they appear in an Aerofilms view of 1965. Alongside the viaduct road across the old Pier district, is the dim shape of Victoria Dwellings, the town council's first attempt at building artisans' homes for working class families. Standing close to the railway line from Folkestone to Dover Priory Station, these five-storey flats had become unfit to live in. I recall being shown conditions there before demolition and feeling the building shake as trains passed by. The steamer leaving is the *Invicta*. The train ferry dock has now been filled in and since 1995 train ferries no longer sail from the port.

The Western Docks in an aerial view from the early 1970s showing, across the centre of the picture, the old viaduct which was soon to be demolished. Victoria Dwellings have gone and a temporary bridge carries traffic to Limekiln Street. In the foreground is the Train Ferry Dock and Southern House. Nearby are council homes in Beach Street and the Seven Star Street flats, both later demolished. Behind is Archcliffe Fort, the Avo factory, Harbour School and Limekiln Street, where more homes were demolished in the 1990s to build the new A20.

The *Shepperton* train ferry, one of three sister ships launched in 1934 with a capacity of twelve sleeping-cars and two baggage cars, or forty rail wagons and 500 passengers. On the right is the pump-house which could raise the level of water in the dock to bring the vessel's train deck up to the level of the dockside railway lines. Adjoining was a car ramp link to the ship's upper-deck garage. Later the garage became passenger accommodation.

The Eastern Docks around 1952 with the first two roll-on, roll-off car ferry berths when they opened. On the left is the ferry *Compiegne* and, on the right, the 1924 *Dinard*, which was converted. Capt. Stuart Townsend started a car ferry service in 1928 from the Camber carrying fifteen cars a trip, each owner paying a £4 7s return. The converted minesweeper *Forde* doubled capacity in 1930. Cars were craned aboard because there were no suitable ramps, yet road vehicles and trains had been driven on and off Port Richborough ferries in 1918.

Townsend Brothers' SS *Forde* alongside the Eastern Arm at the Camber. She was replaced in 1949 by the *Halladale*, another converted naval vessel. From 1931 the *Forde* had a railway-owned competitor, the *Autocarrier*. The old Camber has now been filled in and the dock area considerably extended. Tourist vehicles are predicted to rise to 4.5 million a year by 2010 and freight vehicles to 2.4 million.

This oil painting of Dover Bay is said to depict the return of King Charles II to Britain on his restoration to the throne on 25 May 1660. For years it was owned by the Mowll family, and it still adorned a wall of a lawyer's Dover office as the year 2000 dawned. Both of Dover's Roman pharos towers, one on either side of the valley, are shown. The painting was copied for the British Museum by Dover photographer Charles Harris.

Dover sailing-packet the *King George*, in service between Dover and Calais from 1813 to 1823, depicted in a 1949 painting by Gordon Ellis. The painting was based on a detailed model in Dover Museum, the identity of which was once lost. The *King George* was soon outpaced by the first cross-Channel steamers: the first steamer to cross is believed to have been the 81ft *Rob Roy* of 90 tons, in 1820.

The Promenade around 1890 photographed by entrepreneur Francis Frith (1822-1898) who set out to make a complete photographic record of the British Isles. Today his thousands of negatives form the Francis Frith Collection. On the left is the Grand Hotel which was badly damaged by shelling in the Second World War. It is at right angles to blocks of terraced homes which occupied the site where the Gateway flats now stand. On the hilltop castle church restoration, begun in the mid-1860s, remained unfinished.

The catamaran steamer *Castalia*, of 1875, designed by Capt. W. Dicey of Walmer, was named after the wife of Earl Granville, the Lord Warden of the Cinque Ports. The vessel was supposed to prevent seasickness on the Dover to Calais service. Sadly, the *Castalia* was too slow (11 knots) and was soon withdrawn, becoming an isolation hospital on the River Thames in 1884. It was also in 1875 that Matthew Webb became the first cross-Channel swimmer and the steamer *Bessemer,* which appears elsewhere in this book (on page 69), came to Dover.

The Wellington Dock around 1929, showing sea front homes and offices up to the Esplanade Hotel in the foreground. In the early 1900s the railway from the Western Docks to a liner terminal on the Prince of Wales Pier ran between the properties. In the centre is the Sailors' Bethel corner of Northampton Street, which tramway cars had to negotiate to enter Snargate Street. The *Dinard* is believed to be at Union Street Quay, while the *Maid of Kent* is moored on Gun Wharf to the right of the photograph.

The *Calais Douvres* arrived at Dover in May 1878. The second of two catamarans, but with more powerful 4,000hp engines and two complete hulls, the *Calais-Douvres* was the more successful and popular of the two, carrying up to 1,000 passengers in comfort. But she cost 40 tons of coal a day to run and was too slow. In the winter months it was uneconomical to run her. Withdrawn in 1887 she ended up as a coal hulk.

The *Bessemer* in the Granville Dock, *c.* 1875. This remarkable steamer was designed by Henry Bessemer, made famous for inventing a steel making process. The *Bessemer* had four giant paddle-wheels with what should have been a floating saloon for passengers, with a unique mechanism to absorb the motion of the waves. She was 350ft long and 60ft across the paddle-boxes but capable of only 11 knots. This steamer badly damaged Calais Pier on her first official trip. She was a disaster and was scrapped in 1879.

The Western Docks in the 1880s showing George Hammond's warehouses on Union Street Quay. The company was still a major force as the new millennium dawned. The smaller paddle-steamers on the left were scrapped or sold after the amalgamation of railway companies serving the port. They were Samphire class (336 tons) *Wave, Breeze* and *La France* (1864-1899) while the larger vessel could be the *Prince Imperial*. In Granville Dock is the catamaran *Calais-Douvres*.

Cross-Channel steamers at Union Street Quay in Wellington Dock, *c.* 1900. A horse-drawn bus is about to cross the swing bridge where a sign asks drivers to keep to the right. Presumably pedestrians used the other side. About this time two rival railway companies were merging services to and from the Channel ports. On the far right is the *Lord Warden I*, behind which is the Pentside Baptist Mission.

A striking sailing vessel, the *Leda*, pictured in 1901 discharging sawn timber in the Granville Dock. Earl Granville, the Lord Warden of the Cinque Ports, opened the dock in 1874. George Amos (1827-1914) and his son, Eugene (1872-1942) photographed many such vessels, and took a special interest in ships, rowing out to meet them. Many of their photographs and glass plate negatives are held in various archives.

A turbine-steamer the *Arromanches* enters port through the eastern entrance on 7 March 1950, bringing the President of the French Republic on a state visit to see King George VI and Queen Elizabeth. The aerial rope-way along the Eastern Arm of the harbour, seen behind the ship, brought coal about 6 miles across country from Tilmanstone Colliery to a huge bunker for discharge into ships. In the foreground is part of the Breakwater.

S.S. "Deutschland" at Prince of Wales Pier. Dover.

Atlantic liner the *Deutschland*, one of the world's largest ships of her time, arriving in July 1904 to land and take on passengers at a liner terminal at the Prince of Wales Pier. This Hamburg-Amerika line vessel dwarfs the little station building. The first liner to call at Dover had been the *Prinz Waldemar*. Red Star vessels also called but harbour construction made it difficult for big liners to berth safely and after two years, and two bad incidents, they stopped using Dover on a regular basis.

Five

Cavalcade of History

An etching by William Woollett depicts King Charles II welcomed back to England at Dover beach on his restoration to the throne on 25 May 1660. The site of the landing, where workmen constructed a 'bridge' to assist the royal party, is now a car park between Townwall Street and Camden Crescent. The King was greeted by the mayor Thomas Browne and local cleric John Reading from whom he accepted the gift of a bible. Ten years later, during a two-week stay at Dover Castle, he signed a secret treaty with the French king.

Dover Haven on 31 May 1520 when King Henry VIII sailed to meet the King of France on the Field of the Cloth of Gold. The original painting is at Windsor Castle. The two round towers were near the old Elizabeth Street railway crossing. Seven years earlier the King, after some time at the castle, said goodbye to the Queen and sailed to Calais escorted by vessels of his Cinque Ports fleet. His father, King Henry VII, who appointed him Lord Warden, crossed the Channel from Dover with an army in 1492.

A banquet given in honour of the Duke of Wellington by the town in 1839 was held in a big pavilion opposite Dover's Maison Dieu. The 'Iron Duke', Lord Warden from 1829 to 1852, took a special interest in Dover. A hundred men took 60 days to build the richly decorated 20,000 sq ft structure said to seat 2,250, including 600 women in the galleries who were served 'lighter refreshments'. The feast, held on 30 August 1839, was attended by many statesmen, Barons of the Cinque Ports and members of the aristocracy. The Earl of Guilford gave two 'fat bucks' for roasting.

On 6 February 1840 Prince Albert crossed from France aboard the steam packet *Ariel*, escorted by HMS *Firebrand*, to wed Queen Victoria. The future Prince Consort stayed the night at the York Hotel before preparations for the wedding. Two years later the Queen and Prince Albert toured Dover in a carriage while guests of the Duke of Wellington at Walmer Castle. This picture is one of a set of postcards sold by the *Dover Chronicle*.

Prime Minister Lord Palmerston rides from Castle Street into the Market Square on the day he was installed as Lord Warden in 1861. The ceremony took place at the Bredenstone, a remnant of a Roman pharos which had recently been discovered on the Western Heights. Advanced in years, Lord Palmerston did not devote much time to the ports. His administration abolished tolls on shipping which had financed the maintenance of Dover Harbour since the reign of Queen Elizabeth I. Dover Harbour Board then took charge.

An Easter review of metropolitan volunteer corps mustered nearly 24,000 men at Dover on Easter Monday 1867. Volunteers were joined by regular soldiers of the Royal Artillery and several other regiments for a sham fight involving forts and batteries of Dover Castle and a strong naval force. This included these two steamships which 'attacked' forts and gun batteries. This engraving is from the *Illustrated London News* of 4 May 1867.

Volunteers at the 1867 Easter Monday review march up Castle Hill to the review ground watched by a crowd which included the craftsmen who built several welcome arches across streets in Dover. Troops left London by special trains at 5 a.m. but it was 10 a.m. before all 20,000 men arrived. The Duke of Cambridge took the salute at a march past before the exercise began. The scenario was that an enemy force, backed by ships, was attempting to seize the castle and port.

A welcome arch constructed in Biggin Street for an Easter military and naval exercise on 30 March 1869. On top of the arch stand four men who helped to build it. A banner says 'Welcome Volunteers' with patriotic verses on either side. On the reverse side, seen elsewhere in this book (on page 2), the soldiers are described as 'Our Defenders'. The premises of Penn Bros., cabinet-makers, furnishers and undertakers, are on the left through the central arch. The Lord Warden, William Pitt, had invited men to join a force of defence volunteer companies called fencibles and, in 1798, 329 men served in different units in St Mary's parish.

Another welcome arch at New Bridge on 14 July 1883, part of the decorations for the visit of the Duke of Connaught, brother of King Edward VII, and the Duchess of Connaught. They came to open two local landmarks which were named after them: the newly-built Connaught Hall, at the town hall in Biggin Street, and the popular Connaught Park, on the slopes below Dover Castle. Note the attractive public clock, later sold and no longer in Dover.

The Market Square and King Street with the Fountain Inn, on the right, decorated for the visit of the Duke and Duchess of Connaught. Apart from the former general post office, practically all the buildings on the left have gone and the sites have been redeveloped. The London, County and Westminster Bank, later built on the Fountain site, was badly damaged in the Second World War but, as the year 2000 dawned, it became Bradford & Bingley Building Society offices.

Bench Street, looking towards Igglesden's bakery in the Market Square, decorated for the Duke and Duchess of Connaught's visit. The white building in the centre once housed the offices of the *Dover Chronicle*, and next door was Thompson's chemists, now a restaurant. On the right is Metcalf & Mayes' drapers shop. In recent times both Frederick Greenstreet, maker of high-class riding-boots for many years, and the New Bridge post office traded here.

The Market Square on 14 July 1883. The Palace and Hippodrome on the west side of the square began life as the Empire Theatre of Varieties, opening at the Phoenix Tavern on the left. This photograph was taken on the day the Duke and Duchess of Connaught opened the newly built Connaught Hall and Connaught Park. The theatre and tavern, devastated by a fire, have long since been demolished.

The Market Square in 1891 when the Marquis of Dufferin and Ava became Lord Warden. In 1891 there were three Lord Wardens: Earl Granville and his successor W.H. Smith MP both died in office, and this led to the appointment of the Marquis. Pencester Road is named after a predecessor, Sir Stephen de Pencester who took over as Lord Warden after Prince Edward, later King Edward I, resigned to go to the crusades. One of his important jobs was to rid the Channel of pirates.

Blanchard and Jeffries set off from Dover on their historic balloon flight across the Channel on 7 January 1785, over 120 years before Louis Bleriot flew his aeroplane across. Silence reigned among spectators until Mr Blanchard got so far from the cliff as to be over the sea. He then stood up and saluted spectators, bowing and taking off his hat as he waved his ensign. Then the crowd cheered. The balloonists descended in the Forest of Felmores 12 miles inside France.

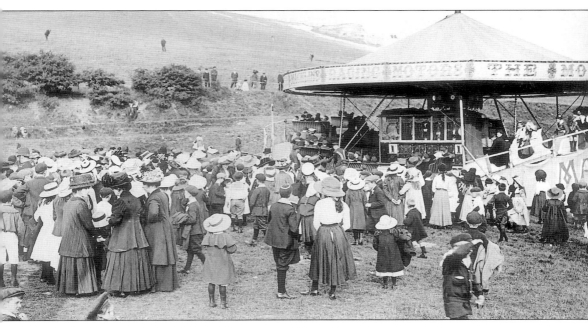

A children's festival treat at Northfall Meadow in 1911, marking the Coronation of King George V and Queen Mary. The population of Dover was 43,647 and the twenty-nine schools had about 9,000 pupils. Of these, 8,900 formed up in Pencester Road to march to the meadow led by police on horseback and preceded by the mayor and councillors. The first children arrived at the meadow before the last left Pencester Road. The popular attraction shown is Macklin's Racing Motors roundabout.

Children of all ages, each wearing a ribbon to identify their school, were joined at Northfall Meadow for the 1911 festival treat by parents pushing younger brothers and sisters in more than 800 prams! Attractions included a Punch and Judy show, a massive tea-party and every child received a special Coronation medal, supplied by Cromwell Marsh, a Dover jeweller, and inscribed with the name of the mayor, Sir William Crundall.

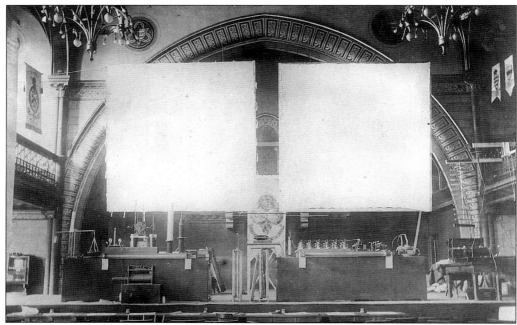

Marconi's radio equipment in Dover Town Hall in 1899. Two years earlier the *Dover Express* had revealed that Gugliemo Marconi was conducting radio experiments, assisted by the Royal Engineers at Fort Burgoyne, near the castle, with wireless stations at Swingate and St Margaret's Bay. With his apparatus Marconi transmitted messages 12 miles to the South Goodwin lightship and later to Wimereux, in France. Members of the British Association witnessed the historic moment as Marconi sent messages to France.

The *Preussen*, the pride and joy of Germany and the world's largest sailing-ship, lies wrecked on the rocks at Fan Bay, not far from the Eastern Arm, in October 1910. The five-masted steel vessel collided with the *Brighton*, a passenger steamer. Holed and taking in water the *Preussen* was taken in tow by three tugs but, sadly, she lost anchors and cables in a gale. The tugs could not hold her, and she was swept onto rocks past Dover and became a total wreck.

The King's birthday parade at Dover sea front in 1910, a time when the town had a large garrison. The previous autumn King George V, who as Prince of Wales briefly held office as Lord Warden during 1906-1907, laid a stone on the Eastern Arm marking the official opening of the Admiralty Harbour. Note the Promenade Pier on the right where the King alighted from a naval launch in 1915 to visit the base and lunch with Admiral Sir Reginald Bacon. (Photograph by Amos & Amos)

King George V and Queen Mary at Dover on 8 May 1922 when they joined the royal yacht for a state visit to the King and Queen of the Belgians and to see the graves of Allied troops of the First World War. The Lord Warden and Lord Lieutenant of Kent met the royal train. Fourteen years later the port saw a succession of the crowned heads of Europe and other world leaders coming to Britain to pay tribute to the late King George V.

83

The memorial to Matthew Webb who, in 1875, became the first person to swim the Channel. The bust was unveiled on Dover sea front in June 1910 by Lord Desborough (W.H. Grenfell) who had stroked an Oxford eight which rowed from Dover to Calais in 1885. Among the guests were Matthew Webb's brother, W.H. Webb, and his cousin Mr Ward, two of those who had accompanied him on the swim. John Bavington Jones, the editor of the *Dover Express*, also witnessed the swim that took Webb 21 hours and 45 minutes.

Fast motor launches of the Royal Navy's Dover Patrol in the Camber during the First World War. The crews of the Dover Patrol performed many acts of heroism in two world wars. This area has now been filled in to extend the Eastern Docks ferry terminal which handles an ever growing volume of vehicles and passengers travelling to and from the Continent, the numbers running into millions every year.

The *Vindictive*, a relic of the epic raid on the German-occupied port of Zeebrugge during the First World War, pictured after the battle when two block-ships were used to bottle up twelve submarines and twenty-three torpedo craft in a Zeebrugge canal on 22 April 1918. The cost was approximately 200 dead and many wounded. Dover Patrol leader Vice-Admiral Roger Keyes was knighted following this raid. The *Vindictive* was in action again on 9 May 1918, this time as a block-ship in a bid to hamper German naval operations at Ostend.

Mayor Richard Barwick rings the Zeebrugge Bell, a relic of the epic attack by the Dover Patrol on the German-held port in 1918. The St George's Day ceremony was held at St Mary's parish church for several years in the early 1920s, but soon switched to the town hall where the bell hangs on a balcony. From left to right: Town Sergeant J. Chapman, Town Clerk R. Knocker, Alderman James Bussey, Mr Barwick, Sir Edwin Farley, Alderman Charles Sellens, Canon W. Elnor, Chief Constable Charles Green, the Town Crier and Town Messenger.

A Royal Navy battleship squadron and torpedo flotilla in Dover's Admiralty Harbour, c. 1910. This massive harbour was officially opened in 1909, but was never fully developed because it was realized that Royal Navy ships would be too vulnerable in wartime to attack from an

Members of the 1908 Dover Pageant included many leading local figures, among them the Earl and Countess of Guilford who are standing in the centre of this group dressed as King Edward I and Eleanor of Castille. One of the biggest events held in Dover, this pageant was staged at the

enemy-occupied France. Admiralty Harbour proved its worth to the Dover Patrol in the First World War, and to the British Expeditionary Force in the Second World War during its evacuation from Dunkirk when the Germans swept through France in 1940.

ancient Dover Priory, the site for over a century of Dover College. There were 2,000 performers, and 600 women and men made costumes and armour, period weapons and banners. The preparations took eighteen months to complete. Pageant Master was Louis Parker.

Lavish decorations for the installation of the Marquis of Willingdon as Lord Warden on 30 July 1936. A former MP of Hastings, he had a mounted escort of 1st Royal Dragoons. Guards of Honour were formed by the 5th (Cinque Ports) Bn Royal Sussex Regt, Royal Marines and Royal Navy, while hundreds of soldiers of the 1st Bn Royal Scots, 2nd Bn Devonshire Regt, 2nd Bn Seaforth Highlanders, the Royal Air Force and members of TA regiments lined the route.

An artist's impression of the Burlington Hotel around 1893. Facing the sea and Promenade Pier directly opposite, the hotel was built on the site of a mansion belonging to the Rice banking family. Mr Henry Rice and his son Edward Royds Rice were both bankers and had trade connections with the Rothschilds. Edward, whose wife Elizabeth was a niece of Jane Austen, was Dover's Liberal MP for twenty years. An influential woman, Mrs Henry Rice was respectfully referred to as 'Madam' Rice. The Burlington Hotel, with its fine ballroom, closed as a hotel in 1924.

Granville Gardens pictured in their heyday, around 1910, with bandstand and glass-roofed conservatory style dance floor and café. Hundreds of people are relaxing in deck-chairs to listen to the band. Above the café can be seen the top of the pavilion at the end of the old Promenade Pier which, sadly, was demolished in 1927. The Grand Hotel stood off the picture to the left. Both hotel and gardens were wrecked during the Second World War.

The Promenade Pier around 1905, looking towards the staging for building the Breakwater, part of the Admiralty Harbour on the left. The pier, in the centre of the Promenade opposite the Burlington Hotel, was opened by a private company in 1892 and had a chequered history. A fine amenity with a concert hall, it was not a financial success. The pier was twice damaged by Royal Navy ships which used it during World War One and, after briefly resuming a leisure role, it finally closed in 1926.

'Britannia, Allies and Peace': members of Wiggins Teape's Crabble Mill staff in fancy dress present a peace tableau in the 1919 carnival, celebrating the end of the First World War. They include Annie Aldridge, Alice Bennet, Nellie Allan, Hilda Plant, Rose Gill, Rachel Kelby, Elsie Powell, Annie Plant, Nellie Hadlow, Corrie King, Dolly Ashurst, May King, T. Edwards, Rose English, Mary Murphy, Queenie Ridgewell, Lily Oyle, May Collins, Maud Edwards, Miss Lyus, Hilda Dyer, George Dovey, 'Daddy' Charles Ashdown and driver Wally Graves.

King Fuad of Egypt arrives at Dover Marine Station on 4 July 1927 for a state visit to Great Britain. Arriving in the steamer *Maid of Orleans*, which flew the Egyptian flag and was escorted by four destroyers and the RAF, King Fuad was greeted by a 21 gun salute from Dover Castle. The Prince of Wales, seen here on the right wearing a busby, welcomed King Fuad who then inspected British Army and Navy Guards of Honour at the pier. Behind the dignitaries are the Pullman coaches of the royal train.

Princess Marina is greeted with a kiss by Prince George, the Duke of Kent, on her arrival at Dover in November 1934, eight days before their wedding. History was made as the daily newspapers installed portable Belingraphe telegraphic transmitting equipment at the local post office for their photographers to use to send images like this one speedily back to their picture desks. A *Star* photographer used a *Dover Express* dark-room to process his picture for the afternoon edition.

Clarendon Street celebrates either the Silver Jubilee of King George V and Queen Mary in 1935, or the Coronation two years later of King George VI and Queen Elizabeth, now the Queen Mother. Note that car, the only one owned by anyone in the street! The same potted aspidistras also appeared in a party picture taken when residents celebrated the Coronation. This photograph was taken from the Belgrave Road end of the street by Farringdon & Harrison.

Flags and bunting decorate Cannon Street to mark the Coronation of King George VI and Queen Elizabeth in May 1937. St Mary's parish church is set back, off to the right. All traces of the old tramway system, which closed down at the end of 1936, have disappeared. On the left a Huntley & Palmer van delivers goods either to the Metropole Hotel bars, the Plaza Cinema, or next door to International's, the grocers.

King George VI inspecting troops of the Royal Artillery when he paid a visit to the Dover Garrison on 10 April 1940. The inspection took place at the small parade-ground between the pharos and the slope that leads up to the Great Keep of Dover Castle. (The writer is glad he didn't have such an ancient .303 rifle, or such a long bayonet, when he did his share of square-bashing during National Service in the Royal Signals!)

Barrage balloon site at Granville Gardens, facing the sea front, in this 1943 photograph from the Imperial War Museum archives. Off to the left a lorry carried gas cylinders used to inflate the balloon. In the background in Townwall Street are the Granville Hotel, Alex Bottle's chemists shop, the Chandos public house, E. Garlinge's confectionery shop and the Robin Hood Inn on the corner of St James' Lane. RAF barrage-balloon personnel were based at St Alphege House in Frith Road.

Home Guardsman Jack Wood, far left, with tin-hatted ARP man Cyril Souton of Hougham, second left, and captured Luftwaffe pilot Artur Dau, still holding his parachute, on the hills above Dover during the Battle of Britain. Dau was shot down on 28 August 1940 by Squadron Leader Peter Townsend, RAF, a distinguished member of 'The Few'. Taking particulars is PC Hills. When Winston Churchill was visiting the command centre under Dover Castle he saw a dogfight and went to see a German plane that crashed at Church Whitfield.

Sixty or more vessels were in Dover Harbour on the last day of the evacuation of our troops from Dunkirk in 1940. Some of these ships are pictured here at the Admiralty Pier landing thousands of grateful troops and airmen rescued from the coast of France. The masts of many sailing-barges that took supplies to the troops during the rescue can be seen above the Prince of Wales Pier in the background.

Three telephone operators, Walter Garrett, George Kerry and John Parfitt, were killed as three shells hit the town on 28 June 1943 partly destroying the exchange in Priory Street adjoining the main post office. A second shell hit houses in Priory Road, three of them collapsing into the street. Ambulance driver William Golding was killed, two soldiers were badly wounded and four other people were slightly hurt. The previous day a shell burst in Cannon Street outside Burton's, and Plaza Cinema film-goers became victims, with one Wren, eleven servicemen and a young girl killed.

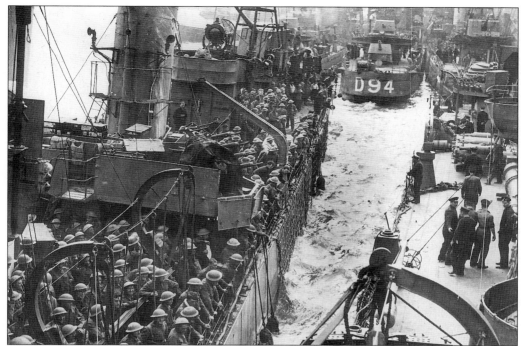

Soldiers pack destroyer the *Icarus* like sardines as it edges alongside another ship berthed at the Admiralty Pier on 31 May 1940. In the rear are more destroyers, including D94, HMS *Whitehall*. In nine days a remarkable armada of ships, large and small, snatched 338,680 British and Allied servicemen from the French coast in the face of invading Germans. At its peak, numbers evacuated in one day were: 29 May, 50,331; 30 May, 53,227; 31 May, 64,141 and 1 June, 61,557.

Burlington Mansions, near the sea front, smashed by bomb and shell. Three people died on 7 September 1941 when this former hotel was hit by three bombs dropped by a Junkers dive-bomber. The victims were caretakers Mr and Mrs Turner and Special Constable William Horn who was the manager of Peppin's tailors in Biggin Street. Shocked and embarrassed were butcher Albert Decourt and his wife. Mr Decourt was left with his trousers down as both lavatory floor and pan disappeared beneath him!

The Guildhall Vaults public house at the corner of Queen Street and Bench Street was destroyed on 4 October 1943 by enemy guns in retaliation for an attack launched by our coastal guns on an enemy convoy. Also damaged was the old Dover Oyster Depot of Ingram Newman in Queen Street (right), shops in King Street and Bench Street and Flashman's furniture depository in Dieu Stone Lane. Notices went up warning thieves about penalties for looting.

Queen Elizabeth, later the Queen Mother, inspects an Aycliffe air-raid warden's post on 18 October 1944. King George VI and Queen Elizabeth visited Dover to mark the end of shelling by long-range guns across the Channel. The capture of these guns was a major objective of Allied forces after the D-Day landings in Normandy. Canadian troops played a vital role in silencing the big gun batteries which had caused many deaths and injuries and much destruction in the town.

In 1944 Dover experienced its worst shelling as German gunners, attacked by invading Canadian troops, delivered a vicious final onslaught using up their ammunition. This is Castle Street on 26 September 1944 where the last shell to fall smashed Pickford's removers and Hubbard's umbrella shop. At Barwick's Cave, Durham Hill, an armour-piercing shell cut through chalk and concrete killing Patience Ransley, aged sixty-three. Across the Channel the Allies took 29,945 prisoners.

King George VI inspects a Guard of Honour of Dover fire officers, including Leading Firewoman Miss Violet Warman, third from the right, outside the town hall on 18 October 1944. Accompanying the King are Mrs Elizabeth Favell, Assistant Group Officer in the town, and the mayor. Also present but out of view was the Queen with her lady-in-waiting. Firewomen on parade included Betty Jolin (later Grossmith), Evelyn Relf, Tillie Beney, Flora Friend, Marion Sewell and Marjorie Brenchley, to quote their maiden names.

Sir Winston Churchill, installed as Lord Warden on 14 August 1946 at Dover College, seen here going to a service at St Mary-in-the-Castle. Afterwards, in an open car, he saluted and gave his famous victory sign to massed crowds in the streets. Later, in the Maison Dieu, he recalled his wartime visits to the castle and other defence positions, observing that he had already acted as 'warden' through five years of war.

Sir Winston Churchill, moved by the great welcome he received, poses for the press in front of the war memorial in Biggin Street in August 1951when he was made an Honorary Freeman of Dover. The older photographer kneeling with his camera, a trifle thin on top, is Stan Wells, a former colleague of the author. He was sports editor of the *Dover Express* for many years and briefly, before his untimely death, the editor of the newspaper.

Ocean racing off the Eastern Arm on 17 June 1950. The leading vessel and eventual winner is *Benbow*, ahead of *Erivale*, in the Royal Ocean Racing Club's 480-mile race to Kristiansand. The massive structure on the pier is the coal staithe from which Kent coal was loaded into ships.

Field Marshal Viscount Montgomery, the hero of the desert war in North Africa when the Desert Rats defeated Rommel. Affectionately known as 'Monty' he is pictured at Dover College on 9 March 1946 when he received the honorary freedom of the town. Guests included other war heroes honoured by Dover, including Admiral Lord Mountevans ('Evans of the Broke' of First World War fame), and Dover VC Thomas Gould RN, another freeman of the town. Centre is college headmaster G.R. Renwick. In a tribute to the town's wartime workers Monty told of his conviction that any German invaders landing in Dover would have been annihilated.

Dover High Street in 1953 lined on both sides by small shops colourfully decorated with bunting to celebrate the Coronation of Her Majesty the Queen. Traffic was two-way and horses and carts still delivered coal and greengrocery. The celebrations, with many street parties, lasted three weeks. In the distance are the town hall and United Reformed church. Much has changed and is still changing in Dover's main street.

The Coronation in 1953 was a red-letter day for Dover. The town excelled itself with decorations. This giant crown, photographed by *Dover Express* journalist Terry Sutton MBE, was brilliantly illuminated at night in the Market Square forming a centre-piece. In the background is Igglesden & Graves' restaurant and Flashman's corner. The *Dover Express*, breaking with tradition, splashed an account of the celebrations across the front page which for decades had been devoted to birth, marriage and death announcements and classifieds. Mr Sutton went on to give over fifty years' service to the local paper.

Shops closed, housework ceased and all of Dover turned out to give the Queen a right royal welcome in March 1958 on her return from a state visit to Holland. She arrived at the Prince of Wales Pier in the royal yacht *Britannia*, commanded by Dover-born Terence Lewin. Here the Queen inspects a Guard of Honour of Gordon Highlanders outside the town hall. Above the shops behind them was a banner bearing the message 'Welcome to Dover'.

The Queen and Prince Philip, the Duke of Edinburgh, meet some of the town's leading figures in the town hall in 1958. The Queen is escorted by the Mayor, Alderman Jack Williams. After signing the visitors' book the royal couple drove to Dover Castle passing 'Queen Elizabeth's Pocket Pistol', a sixteenth-century long-barrelled gun. There they met the Deputy Constable of the Castle, Maj.-Gen. W.F.R. Turner, at the Constable's Tower.

Twentieth Century Fox caused a stir in Dover in 1964 filming sequences of the comedy thriller *Those Magnificent Men in their Flying Machines* in and around town. Bathing-huts and tall drying-huts for fishing nets appeared on the beach, classic cars lined the Promenade and Swingate airfield was resurrected opposite the Duke of York's Royal Military School to be used by replicas of early aircraft. Stars, including Terry Thomas, Eric Sykes, Tony Hancock, Sarah Miles and Robert Morley, were joined by 200 local extras.

Princess Margaret with Lord Snowdon at the opening of the hoverport at the Eastern Docks on 31 July 1968. The couple arrived by helicopter at the pad and joined the inaugural 'flight' for the 30-minute crossing. Also present was the inventor of the hovercraft, Sir Christopher Cockerill. The royal couple was given a model of the SRN4 craft for their children. The British Rail Seaspeed service expanded and in October 1978 the Duke of Kent opened a bigger hoverport next to the Prince of Wales Pier.

Several factories were put out of action in May 1965 when a mystery £1 million fire destroyed the old oil mills known as Commercial Buildings, off Limekiln Street. Flames shot 60ft into the air as fifty firemen fought the blaze. During the 1939-1945 war the oil mills were used by troops and the personnel of the Royal Navy's fast motor torpedo boats, gunboats and air-sea rescue craft. George Hammond's shipping offices were later built on the site.

A De Dion Bouton car (Kent registration D-1531) owned by a Dover surgeon is pictured on 26 June 1905 when it was used to take Flora Goldsack of Coldred Court Farm to be married to Alfred John Fisher. Flora Fisher's daughter Gwen Bates of Astley Avenue showed me this picture. The chauffeur at the tiller steering was Charlie Butcher of River, who worked for the car's owner Dr J.L. Rubel of the Red House (now Redlands), London Road, River. The doctor was a family friend.

Her Majesty the Queen Mother is installed as the first ever female Lord Warden of the Cinque Ports at Dover College in August 1979. Sworn into office at the Grand Court of Shepway, the Queen Mother paid tribute to the little ships from around the coast that rescued our troops from the beaches of Dunkirk in 1940. Her ride in the Scottish state coach from Dover Castle, accompanied by Prince Edward and his cousins Viscount Linley and Lady Sarah Armstrong-Jones, was a glittering spectacle.

The late Countess of Guilford, on the left, at the official opening of the Roman Painted House, off York Street, in May 1977. Wearing a hard hat, on the right, is leading archaeologist Brian Philp of Kent Archaeological Rescue Unit, the team which discovered the Roman town house. The walls decorated with coloured plaster were conserved and the archaeologists built a popular museum in which to preserve the finds. In its first three years the award-winning Roman Painted House attracted 100,000 visitors.

Six

Horses to Motors

Horses and carts in King Street, viewed from the Market Square, before the arrival of the Dover Corporation Tramway in 1897. Street lighting was by gas and a variety of lamps can be seen. On the left is Igglesden's bakery and narrow openings into Church Street and Castle Street. The central white building is Binfield Bros wine merchants, and to the left of it is Killick, Back & Sons, drapers.

The Eagle stage-coach at Dover in an 1828 aquatint by H. Alken. Coaching company Chaplin & Co. ran a service from the King's Head and Chaplin's hotels in Dover to the Spread Eagle in Gracechurch Street, London. Other coaches ran from the Worthington family's Ship Hotel on Custom House Quay. In 1837 Henry Worthington had the Eagle Coach Office in Snargate Street. Coaches running between the Royal Oak, Cannon Street, or the Shakespeare Hotel and London took about nine hours! In 1838 it was estimated that 30,000 passengers a year travelled by coach from London to Dover.

Frank Sneller's horse and cart outside a Dover paper-mill where it delivered wood-pulp for paper making. The transport business grew from a butcher's shop opened by Stephen Sneller in De Burgh Street in 1867. It progressed to a horse-drawn bus and grew into a modern transport business with seventeen lorries, some 150hp giants. Stephen's great-grandson Harold Sneller headed a staff of thirty, but in 1979 the firm closed down.

James Link senior of Buckland, a Dover blacksmith for many years, at his Bunker's Hill forge close to Buckland Bridge around 1915. Jimmy (left) with assistant 'Foggy' Fogg, is teaching two soldiers how to shoe a horse. On the right are forge buildings and in the background the Bull public house. James Link, who took over from Charlie Peirce, died in 1963, aged eighty-one. Appropriately, his gravestone at Buckland churchyard has an anvil engraved on it. His son Jimmy, now deceased, took over the Dover business.

George Potter began a business in Worthington's Lane in 1863 to be succeeded by George Potter junior, pictured here with a horse and cart in Ladywell. When one-time councillor Sam Gambles, a partner in the firm, took over in 1924 there were three horses and carts and a model T Ford lorry. By 1968 George Potter Transport Ltd incorporating the business of Baldock & Co. had grown to twenty-four vehicles. In 1969 Thanet Transport Ltd of Ramsgate took over.

A contemporary print shows the first train to leave the Shakespeare Cliff tunnel on the coast-hugging line from Folkestone to Dover which was opened on 6 February 1844. Engineer William Cubitt's men cut four tunnels through the cliffs and a timber causeway across Shakespeare Beach, which was pounded by the sea in bad weather. One tunnel went under Archcliffe Fort. On the railway's opening there was a triumphant parade from New Bridge to the station site near the Admiralty Pier, and a banquet in the Theatre Royal.

The sea front railway, c. 1955. Steam trains once hauled wagon-loads of scrap-iron, coal and oil along the Promenade to or from the Eastern Arm. The line was built on Admiralty orders to link both sides of the harbour and ran from July 1918 until 1964. There were oil-tanks in the cliffs and on the quayside for refuelling ships. The locomotive pictured here passing Waterloo Crescent, No. 31027 a P-class 0-6-0 tank-engine, still runs today on the Bluebell Railway.

The famous boat express train the *Golden Arrow*, being hauled by a Britannia-class 4-6-2 locomotive the *Shakespeare* (No. 70004), is photographed outside Marine Station by former local businessman Harold Sneller as it headed for London in pre-electrification days. Like the *Flying Scotsman*, the *Golden Arrow* was a revered institution. It was expected to reach the Admiralty Pier at Dover from Victoria Station in London in 98 minutes, with passengers reaching Paris in six and a half hours.

Dover Marine Station with the *Ile de France* at the quay, *c.* 1924. The station was built on a massive site reclaimed from the sea in order to widen the Admiralty Pier immediately after the Admiralty Harbour was completed in 1909. It was 1913 before work on Marine Station began. The terminus of the famous *Golden Arrow* for many years, the station building now has a new role as part of a cruise liner terminal. Preserved features include a fine memorial to the railwaymen who lost their lives serving in two world wars, but the railway link has gone.

Willard Sawyer, a Dover carpenter and leading bicycle builder, who exhibited at the 1851 Crystal Palace exhibition. Customers for his four-wheel 'velocipedes' included the Prince of Wales, the Russian emperor and the Prince Imperial of France. Sawyer had premises in St James Street, Dover, and St George's Street, Deal. The Crystal Palace machine is thought to be the one preserved in the Science Museum. Built partly of wood and propelled with foot treadles, it cost £30. Sawyer is pictured on a four-wheeler with a studio backdrop of the Dover heights.

A John Fowler traction-engine hauling five wagons in Dover in the late nineteenth century. The traction-engine was owned by local haulage firm John Robson who had several McLaren engines and did agricultural contract work with Fowler steam ploughs. The railway embankment behind may be the one taking the track across Crabble Hill. The firm had nine or ten engines, but in 1923 tractors and tackle were sold and George Potter (Transport) Ltd took over the business.

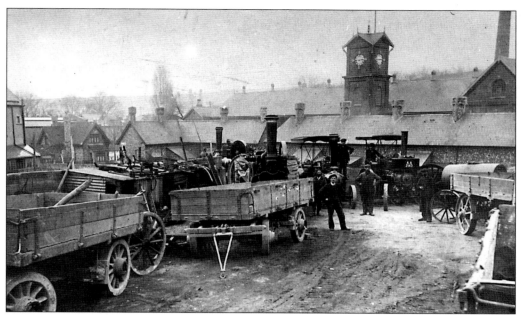

Arthur and George Baldock's traction-engine yard near Wiggins Teape's Buckland paper-mill, seen in the background, at Crabble Hill in the 1920s. The haulage contracting business was founded by their uncle, Arthur Baldock, and later taken over by George Potters. The yard, with an entrance off Old Park Road, stood behind a row of flint cottages on Crabble Hill, where Hollis Motors later had a filling-station.

Steam buses came to Dover in June 1899 to run one of the earliest regular services in the country, to and from St Margaret's-at-Cliffe. The East Kent Motor Bus Co.'s open-fronted wagonette *Pioneer* with vertical steam boiler at the front carried 28 passengers. Capable of about 18mph it was said to take steep gradients in its stride. The run to Bay Hill Coastguard Station took 40 minutes. Parish council chairman Harris Stone headed the company.

Builder William Henry Grigg's car (D-351), nicknamed 'Puffing Billy' by the family, in 1911. Its official registration in 1903 as a 'Humberette with dogcart body' seems to have been cancelled on 31 July 1905. The record was changed to 'Baby Peugeot, 5hp with dogcart body in dark green, weighing 7cwt.' In August 1910 Mr Grigg became the car's owner. He is pictured with his wife outside their home, Salisbury House, in Beaconsfield Road.

Brewer's drays bearing Phoenix emblems on top of the radiators stand outside Alfred Leney's Phoenix Brewery, in Castle Street, Dover in the early part of the twentieth century. Note the heavy gun carriage type wheels with solid tyres and acetylene headlamps. The brewery yard became the site of the Granada (later ABC) Cinema which in turn went on to become a night-club.

Oliver Arter ran the Arter Bros taxi business in Effingham Crescent opposite the town hall. These Unic station landaulettes of around 1914-1918, had acetylene-burning headlamps, a far cry from today's iodine quartz and halogen lights. Mr Arter's brother had a garage and agricultural business on the A2 at Barham. This photograph is from Joe Harman, a former Dover tram conductor and ambulance officer.

Charles Ashdown, furniture remover, undertaker and church worker, with an early Benz car, c. 1900. 'Daddy' Ashdown, pictured outside his Cherry Tree Avenue premises, is believed to have bought the car from a local GP. The first local car owner is thought to have been Major Murray Lawes, of Old Park Mansion, Whitfield, who had a 1898 6hp Daimler (Kent registration number D-53) which still runs in rallies under new ownership.

Charabancs at Town Station, Lord Warden Square, 1910. A party from Hastings has come to visit Guilford Colliery, near Whitfield, and Tilmanstone Colliery. They included shareholders of the company developing the collieries, who had a meeting in the Queen's Hall, Dover, and a ceremony marking the start of a third shaft at Tilmanstone Colliery. The first charabanc is an MMC, the others, with bodies by Maltby Motors of Sandgate, include a Lacoste et Battmann of 1908.

East Kent Road Car Co. buses and charabancs in Tower Hamlets Road engaged for one of the biggest ever Dover excursions in the 1930s. Each Daimler has a plaque indicating an outing run by the Borough Conservative Association. Some of the buses may have had bodies made in George Sacre Palmer's coach works in London Road. (Photograph by G.H. Jarrett)

114

Charabancs ready for a summer outing pose to have their photograph taken on the old A2 just beyond the top of Crabble Hill around 1923-1926. The white gate belonged to the Red House, now flats called Redlands Court. The charabanc on the left (KK4502) is believed to be a French Brasier and that on the right a Dennis. Some charabancs had interchangeable lorry bodies. (Photograph by Charles Harris of Dover, given to the author by Mrs Sylvia Dunford)

Barwick's the builders staff boarding a Pullman charabanc around 1912, part of a fleet of vehicles run by Cheriton proprietor 'Father' Eric Wills, who later sold out to the East Kent Road Car Co. This photograph was taken outside Barwick's original premises in Snargate Street. Sitting in the driver's seat is a very young Robert Barwick, later to become chairman of the building contractor's and a senior magistrate. The charabanc has artillery type wheels with solid tyres.

Dover Tramways car No. 9, with open top, in the Market Square, *c.* 1900. This photograph was taken just before the Garrick's Head public house, Lester's the saddlers and several other small shops came down to build Lloyds Bank. While this work was taking place, part of the crypt of the long-demolished church of St Peter was found. It is believed St Peter's and its churchyard spanned the sites of most of the properties from the Antwerp Hotel behind the tram to Igglesden & Grave's.

English Electric Tram car No. 27 and a Southern Railway P-class 0-6-0 tank-locomotive run side by side in Strond Street, but on different gauge tracks, around 1930. The Wainwright engine hauls assorted goods wagons to Harbour Station, past Holy Trinity church just in front of it on the left. The tram is passing by on the 'wrong' side as it heads for Buckland from the pier. The top cover of the tram was added in 1929.

Tram car No. 3 inside the Maxton terminus 'garage' in the early 1920s where it was rebuilt by the tramway's own craftsmen after many years service. It was scrapped in 1927. George Archer, a tramway worker from 1919-1926, took the picture before joining the East Kent Road Car Co. Pictured are Bill Brooks, George Creed, Bill Fuller, F. Harmer, Andy Knott, Ted Nye, Alf Russ and Ted Sole.

Last tram to Maxton, 31 December 1936. The Dover Corporation Tramway closed in favour of an East Kent Road Car Co. bus service run on terms which kept down the council rates. The last tram was cheered all the way to the Maxton depot where this photograph was taken by Whorwell & Son. Mayor H. Medgett Norman and official driver Percy Sutton are at the controls. To the left of the 'L' plates is tramway inspector Fred Pay who drove the first Maxton tram thirty-nine years earlier.

A Dover-built Rolls-Royce by Palmer's Connaught Coachworks. Palmer's were wheel-wrights and coach builders in Dover from 1875 with workshops in Priory Street and, around 1896, at the corner of London Road and Coombe Valley Road. Craftsmen built bodies on chassis supplied by major manufacturers, including this 20/25hp Rolls-Royce at the Cherry Tree Avenue workshops. It was the last of about a dozen built at Palmer's in the 1930s. Finished cars were towed to Dover Priory Station by horse (!) en route to London said the owner of this photograph, Bert Pain of Whitfield, who worked on this Rolls-Royce.

G.S. Palmer & Son's motor body works staff, March 1909. The coach works provided jobs for around 100 staff. Managing Director Walter Palmer is sitting in the second row seventh from the left, with his wife Julia by his side.

Growth in the volume of traffic led to calls for better access to Lord Warden Square in the 1890s but it was 1922 before the viaduct, on the right, was opened. By the mid-1970s the viaduct needed to be rebuilt and it is pictured fenced off, after a temporary viaduct had been built. In the background is Archcliffe Fort. The Golden Arrow public house (centre) survived when Beach Street and Seven Star Street behind it were demolished.

The Market Square was used as an East Kent Road Car Co. terminus for out of town and Folkestone Road/Elms Vale buses. On the right a Daimler charabanc (FN 4442), one of forty bought new by the company in 1920, awaits passengers for a circular tour. The bus office, on the left, was close to the Carlton Club, the site of the town's first telephone exchange. Bunting signifies an important event such as Cricket Week or the carnival. Tramlines in the foreground indicate the date is pre-1936.

Louis Bleriot and his wife in Northfall Meadow after his historic flight. Flying his little monoplane made of ash and poplar, on 25 July 1909 Louis Bleriot became the first man to fly an aircraft across the Dover Strait. The flight took Bleriot 37 minutes, with the monoplane easily outpacing an escorting destroyer that was carrying his wife. A handful of people saw the plane land in Northfall Meadow, where today the spot is marked by an outline of the plane in concrete.

Charles Rolls, of Rolls-Royce fame, about to set off on the first non-stop two-way flight of the Channel in a Wright Brothers' biplane on 2 June 1910. He took off from behind Dover Castle at Swingate at 6.28 a.m. and dropped greetings to the French at 7.15 a.m. Rolls was sighted approaching Dover again at 7.45 a.m., and landed at about 8 a.m. when police had to hold back a crowd of 3,000. Tragically, Rolls was killed a month later at a Bournemouth air show.

Seven

Townscapes

An aerial view of the sea front around 1931 gives a good impression of the town's development, extending from Pencester Gardens to Marine Parade, before Second World War damage. The roof of the Granada Cinema, opened in 1930, can be seen in Castle Street. In the foreground on the left a visiting fair adds to the attraction of the sea front, with its promenade and pebble beach crowded with visitors.

Marine Parade with its attractive crescent of houses built around 1825. On the left are the Dover Harbour Board Offices and the property that later became the White Cliffs Hotel, now called Churchill's. The sweep of Waterloo Crescent is broken half-way along by the Grand Hotel, set back at right angles, and various gardens. This picture pre-dates the building of the Promenade Pier, which was opened in 1893 and demolished in 1927.

A beach scene in the 1910s when there was still a handsome Promenade Pier in the centre of the bay, with a concert hall at the end of the pier, as well as berths for pleasure-steamers to land and pick up passengers. Note the blocks of three or four-storey houses on the sea front, and the bathing-machines for those who wanted to change into swimming clothes, although to show much more than a bare ankle was illegal.

The Promenade around 1900 showing, from left to right, the old Esplanade Hotel opposite the clock tower, Waterloo Crescent, Granville Gardens and the terraced houses which would become the site of the Gateway flats. This scene remained little changed until the Second World War devastated much of the property. Note the wooden capstans on top of the shingle. On the right, with a balcony and projecting foyer, is the old Royal Cinque Ports Yacht Club.

A panoramic view of the once densely built-up area extending from the allotments above Adrian Street in the foreground, across to the castle. This photograph can be dated to around 1903 by a network of timbers used to build the Southern Breakwater which are just visible on the horizon beyond the Promenade Pier pavilion. On the right is a good view of the 1850s slipway and the synagogue near New Bridge. In the centre are the white Town Mill, the Grand Hotel and the Burlington Hotel, all now demolished, like the synagogue.

The view from the Western Heights around 1905 showing the Promenade Pier (centre) which was opened in 1893 and demolished in 1927, and part of the Prince of Wales Pier (right). On the left is the old military hospital, below which the Avo factory was built overlooking Strond Street and Harbour Station on the right. The Admiralty Harbour is virtually finished but there is no warship in sight.

The harbour as seen from Dover Castle, c. 1905. This view is looking towards the Prince of Wales Pier and the Admiralty Pier, which is being extended as part of the Admiralty Harbour scheme. The Promenade Pier juts out from the Promenade in the centre. A quiet day, there is only one tiny steamer to be seen, dwarfed by the Admiralty Pier. In the foreground are the rooftops of homes called Victoria Park. The Burlington Hotel lift shaft to the right stands high above all the other buildings.

This view of Dover from the Western Heights above Adrian Street was used in an 1869 book on the town, one of the first to incorporate photographs. Snargate Street runs diagonally across the picture and shows a great density of property. Towards the top is the 1850s slipway and on the right is the back of Waterloo Crescent and what is now the Churchill Hotel.

Dover's main estate of prefabs at Buckland is shown here in 1967 not long before their demolition. The town lost nearly 1,000 premises through bombing and shelling in the Second World War, with close on 3,000 severely damaged. About 450 prefabs replaced some of these lost homes. In the distance, in the top left-hand corner, the Green Lane council estate, next door to the Old Park Barracks, is being built. The barracks were the base of the Junior Leaders Regiment of the Royal Engineers.

This view of the Barton Road area around 1880, looking towards Cherry Tree Avenue and Union Road (now renamed Coombe Valley Road) was photographed by George Amos standing on the Dover to Deal railway embankment, a part of the railway line that opened in June 1881. Practically the whole area we know as Barton was then farmland. Behind the dark hedge that runs across the centre of the picture is Barton Road and Buckland Avenue. To the right of centre are the gasworks with tall chimney, Harding's Brewery and William Kingsford's water-mill, later Mannering's Mill. To the left, in the centre, are the Fountain and Cherry Tree public houses.

A townscape viewed from Castle Hill, just above Castlemount School, on the left, around 1890. The New St James' church can be seen in the central foreground and, to the left of it, G. Brace & Sons' Stembrook water-mill in Castle Street. The mill was opposite Alfred Leney's Phoenix Brewery, later the site of the Granada Cinema. Outside of the Admiralty Pier the four funnels of the catamaran steamer *Calais-Douvres* help to date the original picture. The old market hall dominates the Market Square.

Maison Dieu Road, or Castle Estate, *c.* 1900. This photograph was taken from the slopes below Castlemount Secondary School, a site now occupied by modern homes off Castle Avenue. In the immediate foreground is St Paul's Roman Catholic church in Maison Dieu Road, standing opposite a line of large villas which used to front Pencester Road, but have now gone. Beyond the church is Brook House, controversially demolished and replaced by a car park.

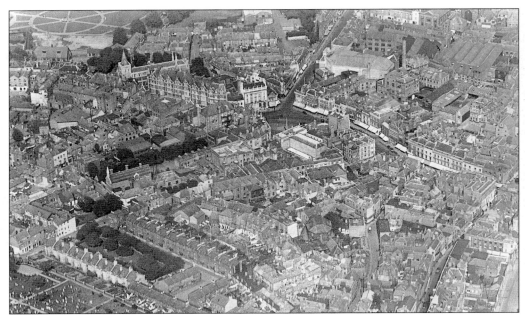

Dover as seen from above the Adrian Street allotments and Cowgate Cemetery, around 1935. Just above the centre of the photograph is the Market Square with the white-fronted façade of Lloyds Bank. Alfred Leney's Phoenix Brewery can still be seen behind the Granada Cinema. Opposite, at Stembrook, is the old tannery. Following war damage and post-war clearance most of the property in the lower half of the picture has gone.

The seaward part of the town in the 1950s, before the Gateway flats were built on the sites of war-damaged properties on Marine Parade. This view is from the top of Adrian Street, on the lower left-hand side. In the central foreground is part of Snargate Street and, on the right, part of New Bridge. Below the crescent of Victoria Park (top left) is the tall chimney of the Phoenix Brewery, off Castle Street. The new A20 now cuts through this area on the right of the photograph.